Transforming the Difficult Child:

True Stories of Triumph

Jennifer Easley
Howard Glasser

Transforming the Difficult Child: True Stories of Triumph

by Jennifer Easley and Howard Glasser

Copyright 2008 by Jennifer L. Easley, M.A, and Howard N. Glasser, M.A.

For information contact:
Howard Glasser
4165 West Ironwood Hill Drive
Tucson, Arizona 85745
E-mail: adhddoc@theriver.com

For orders within the book industry, please contact Brigham Distributing at 435-723-6611.

Cover art by Alice Rose Glasser. Book production assistance provided by Michael Kichler. Copy editing by Chris Howell. Printed by Vaughan Printing, Nashville, TN.

Library of Congress Card Catalogue Number: Pending

ISBN 0-9670507-9-0

Printed in the United States

First Printing: October 2008

To all the Stories of Triumph...those that made it to this volume, those that remain quietly in the background, and those that will be become part of future volumes of Nurtured Heart Approach™ successes. And to all the magnificent efforts, wisdom and determination of all who made these victories of the soul come to life!

ABOUT THIS BOOK

For years now, people have been sending me stories about how the Nurtured Heart Approach™ has contributed to the transformation of their child, family, friends, spouse, classroom, business, self or life in general. People insistently credit me for everything from renewed appreciation of the positive changes in their child to renewed relationships with their children, from a renewed inner life to a renewed marriage or sex life, from a renewed career or business to a renewed relationship with their pet.

The stories keep me energized. (I won't be very surprised if someday I am even credited for someone winning the lottery or having their laundry come out cleaner!)

I have saved these stories with the thought that I might someday compile them into a sort of 'Chicken Soup for the Soul' of Nurtured Heart Approach success stories. Even though each and every success letter has been dear to me and even though I had no trouble envisioning how proud I would be of sharing them, the letters would no doubt have simply remained in the file. But then it occurred to me that this book could have a greater purpose: that of further teaching the approach through the vehicle of these successes. Then I just knew it had to happen.

Approaching Jennifer Easley to do this collaboratively was the best decision ever. As my co-author on *Transforming the Difficult Child: The Nurtured Heart Approach*, which was the original book, she not only knew this approach intimately, but she already had experienced so many of these success stories within her own family and with her clients.

There are three major 'Stands' in the Nurtured Heart Approach, and we began to see that the success stories seemed to fall into, or illustrate perfectly, one of these three Stands. Therefore, we organized these stories, and therefore this book, according to the Stands. And so there are stories where the main lesson is about **taking a stand to energize success**; there are stories about **taking a stand to not energize negativity**; and there are stories about **taking a stand on limits and consequences**. There's also an additional chapter of stories about the approach's transformation capabilities in general – how it has healed so many. Every one of these stories recounts a successful transformation, in many cases submitted from or about people in hopeless situations, some are children and some adults.

As the co-authors of this compilation, Jennifer and I have added commentary after each story. We hope our commentaries will help the reader see 'beyond' the illustrated story – the greater picture of the complex challenges facing families in pretty dire situations. We also offer our commentaries as a way to underscore the inspiration and to open our hearts with gratitude to the heroes of these stories. You'll soon see what we mean.

Most of all, we hope these 'Nurtured Heart' success stories move you – stir your excitement, bring you great joy, and inspire you to transform your own difficult child with the Nurtured Heart Approach.

Following each story is some biographical information provided by the author. Many of these authors also have been kind enough to provide contact information, which you will find on the Contributors page at the back of this book.

Howie Glasser

ABOUT THE AUTHORS

Jennifer Easley is the co-author of two books with Howard Glasser: *Transforming the Difficult Child: The Nurtured Heart Approach* (1999), and now this book. Easley's work as a child and family counselor entered into a new path of higher powered healing when she met and trained with Glasser, the originator of the Nurtured Heart Approach. Not only did his approach return her to the field as a counselor who was burned out, it changed her means of helping families, including her own. Much to Easley's surprise, the approach became critical in raising her own challenging child, who was just an infant when the first book was published.

Easley has 25 years of experience helping children and their families as a nationally certified Master's-level counselor. She has Washington state licensure as a mental health counselor with both child and elder specialties. Rather than providing individual therapy for children, Easley now believes in training and empowering parents as the best and most appropriate healers for their children. She provides in-home and phone counseling as well as Nurtured Heart Approach trainings for small groups, local schools and treatment facilities.

She recently resumed a part-time counseling practice, with new resolve and intent to share the lessons she has learned since becoming a mother. Easley's recent passion is assisting mothers of 'Indigos,' a newer generation of spiritually aware and sensitive children and young adults. She shares Nurtured Heart tenets as well as a blend of native shamanism, Buddhist and Goddess tradition teachings in her current counseling practice. Easley lives on Vashon Island in Washington with her husband Glenn and son Forest Hart. (See the Contributors section for contact information.)

Howard Glasser is the founder of Children's Success Foundation and designer of the Nurtured Heart Approach. He and Jennifer Easley are the co-authors of *Transforming the Difficult Child: The Nurtured Heart Approach* (1999), currently the top-selling book on the topic of ADHD. He is also the author *The Inner Wealth Initiative: The Nurtured Heart Approach for Educators* (2007), currently the top-selling book on school interventions. His latest of five published works is *All Children Flourishing: Igniting the Greatness of Our Children* (2008).

Glasser has been a featured guest on CNN and a consultant for '48 Hours.' He lectures in the U.S. and internationally, teaching therapists, educators, and parents about the Nurtured Heart Approach, which is now being used in hundreds of thousands of homes and classrooms around the world. He has been a consultant for numerous psychiatric, judicial and educational programs. Although he has done extensive doctoral work in the fields of clinical psychology and educational leadership, he feels his own years as a difficult child contributed the most to his understanding of the needs of challenging children and to the success of his approach. Glasser is former Director and Clinical Supervisor of the Center for the Difficult Child in Tucson, Arizona, where he resides.

ACKNOWLEDGMENTS

My primary acknowledgment and appreciation is to Howard Glasser, the most powerful, integral blend of mentor, visionary, teacher and friend. Howie challenged me to rise to my mothering and counseling greatness. Not only did he return me to the helping field, armed with new tools to support greatness, he also helped me in the challenged throes of motherhood.

To my warrior/teacher/son Hart, I hold the deepest gratitude. Hart pulled the biggest veil from my eyes – the mask of the healer needing healing. It took three years in the mother bear cave with him to recognize what was really needed for both of us and our family. Without my powerful son, I could not have done the necessary mother/warrior/healer work to offer our family the biggest steps of strength and joy yet.

To my patient and enduring husband, Glenn, I owe deep, loving thanks as well. Glenn spent many a night waiting up for me as I wrote at the computer, saying "I'm almost finished." He also provided wise, true edits for the story I contributed to this book. Primarily, Glenn has been the rock of stability in the flowing waters of our family's healing journey. He was and continues to be the shore to swim back to as we learned together how to parent Hart with integrity and in support of Hart's many strengths.

My deepest gratitude and heartfelt thanks to my gentle and loving father, William Seward Stotts, who continues to offer support and wisdom regarding the paths of life, heart and helping others.

To further acknowledge, this book represents karmic correction for all the years of strident advice to parents, teachers and care providers struggling with challenging children when childfree myself. After direct experience parenting my own powerhouse son, I now have a newly deepened respect and heightened empathy for those raising or working with challenging children. After some 25 years as a counselor, I realize now that every child, adult, parent and elder I meet is a teacher for me, especially the challenging ones. Special thanks now to those I've worked with, past and present, especially the children. They are the ones leading the way for collective paradigm shifts and healing.

Finally, I have felt so deeply touched and honored to be the 'catcher/collector' of the most incredible stories shared in this book. They are true stories, from the lives of the amazing parents, counselors, educators and professionals who courageously lived and shared them. Their stories are the heart and soul of this book. Heartfelt thanks to them for sharing their wealth and successes and for trusting me to hold and carry these beautiful transformation stories into the world. Specific and profound thanks as well for the creative and stunning support and work of the Nurtured Heart Advanced Trainers who contributed to this project. They continue to amaze and inspire me as the creative torches in this pioneering community. May those daring Nurtured Heart 'pioneers of the positive' forge on and inspire others to do so in their footsteps.

May all who read these true stories of hope and healing seek the high road of gentle strength for the amazing children in all of our care.

Jennifer Easley

I am so grateful to the authors of these stories as well as appreciative of the key players in each. It was so wonderful to have a vehicle to express that gratitude by nature of my commentary after each story, but I feel I cannot come close to expressing all the gratitude in my heart. Each story represents so much great effort, determination, creativity and desire. And each great outcome hopefully will continue to bring great joy and satisfaction to the people involved in each of the stories. You all have shared so deeply from your heart. From your brilliant actions has come a wonderful and precious impact on another human being.

THE SUCCESSES DID NOT JUST HAPPEN, I assure you. Although I brought forth the Nurtured Heart Approach, I do not get the credit. That's because I know the secret: I can share this approach all day long but it doesn't guarantee in the slightest that someone will take the ball and run with it. When push comes to shove, it is only by the efforts and determination of those running with the approach that makes things happen, and without them nothing would happen. To our contributors, I say: These successes are a function of your powerful choices, your great judgment, your inspiring wisdom, your deep caring, and your wonderful willingness to share for the purpose of inspiring those reading this book. Congratulations on having these great qualities and more.

I am so grateful to the magnificent efforts of Jennifer Easley in making this book a reality. Her talents as a 'midwife' to these stories reflect so many magnificent skills. Most stories needed a bit or more of polishing, an enhancement of the details. Jenn somehow was the just the right person with the knack for that and gave the idea for this book just the inspiration and touches it needed. Jenn is a great friend and a miracle in my life.

I am also so grateful to Chris Howell's great talent for editing. Once again she skillfully helped to bring yet another project together – in this case a task of great magnitude. She has an amazing talent for knowing the best road to take from a reader's point of view and knowing just what needs to be done to make everything shine. Thanks so much, Chris, for your brilliance.

Great gratitude also to designer Michael Kichler for creating the look of this book. You are so talented and so great to work with.

Once again I am also able to add great gratitude for my wonderful daughter Alice's contribution for supplying the artwork for the cover. This is her third painting that I am so honored to have forever linked to my work.

And thank you so much to Susan McLeod, who took my breath away with the story and glory she shares with us in the Foreword. I absolutely love the trajectory of her vision and love what she brings forth in support of those learning and using the Nurtured Heart Approach through her EnergyParenting.com.

Lastly I want to thank the growing number friends and colleagues who believe in the Nurtured Heart Approach and who live the approach in their homes, classrooms, practices and within their own hearts. You continue to inspire my life and always will.

Howard Glasser

TABLE OF CONTENTS

FOREWORD

The day is etched clearly in my mind: that day I sat down to read *Transforming the Difficult Child: The Nurtured Heart Approach*, by Howard Glasser and Jennifer Easley. Before my behind even hit the chair, my eyes were consuming the words like a ravenous she-bear. You see, things weren't how I wanted them at home. I dreamed my whole life of being a mother. Not just a 'good enough' mom. My heart's desire was to be the kind of mom who gives her children roots and wings and is the soil and wind. But that's not how things were turning out, and it was wrenching my heart and turning my life upside down.

Then, just a paragraph or two into Page 1 of the book, my pace slowed. I started taking in each word. Then I stopped, went back and re-read the paragraph. It was the description of a 4-year-old boy, Brandon, a boy just like my then 4-year-old son, and the ensuing story of how his parents turned him around with the approach. In that instant, faith filled my heart. I simply knew in my inner being that this approach was the answer to my desperate cry for help to raise my challenging child.

My son, whom I now delightedly refer to as a 'formerly difficult child,' uses his energy and intelligence beautifully. He is a gift – to himself, to his family, to his teachers and to the world – and I now have the tools and skills to parent him no matter what our future holds.

Reading Brandon's story was an important part of that remarkable turnaround. If a picture paints a thousand words, then a story touches a million lives. I identified with Brandon's story and with his parent's story, and that connection was the doorway to my own family's story of transformation.

The book you now hold in your hands is filled with stories that pinpoint life-changing turning points. These are stories that will enlarge your vision, encourage your heart and entreat your soul to join in the sacred mission of igniting a child's greatness. Who among us can't recall being the innocent child seeking the answer to that larger-than-life question, "Who am I?" Many of us – dare I say most of us? – are perhaps well into our second childhood and still seeking the fullness of the answer for ourselves. As adults, all of our interactions with children serve to help them formulate their own answer to that pressing question. It is a powerful position of influence with far-reaching effects and must not be shrugged off as if it is not.

The Nurtured Heart Approach™ opens the eyes of our own hearts and teaches us to use our energy with awakened consciousness and for a higher purpose. It is designed to help us demonstrate to the child – over and over and over again – that the answer to all worthwhile questions is "I am" instead of "I am not."

Recall the age-old trick we adults use like second nature in matters of less importance, such as teaching a child to swim. There's that moment when the child says, "Don't let go of me! I can't swim without your hand under me." To which the parent, who had removed his hand some moments prior, says, "Son, you've been swimming on your own already." And the child internalizes: "I can swim." "I am swimming." "I swam." "I AM a swimmer."

But to use that trick to pull a child into his or her greatness by reflecting the irrefutable makings of strong character, high values and unique gifts – this is the beckoning of the Nurtured Heart Approach.™ It calls us to walk the parental path far beyond birthing a child's physical body, empowering us to continue in the co-creative call to raise a child to his or her brightest and highest expression of self. You'll read examples of it time and time again in these pages, and your heart will enlarge in response. How could one resist when, thanks to the gift of the Nurtured Heart Approach,™ the path is laid out so surely, so simply, and strewn with the gift of witnessing the most precious moments of life?

There are so many children in surroundings that reflect and magnify their worst and direct them to abandon their sacred birthright of greatness. You'll be reading about some of them in this book. But let me clue you in: they all have happy endings thanks to the skillful application of the Nurtured Heart Approach.™

It is never too late for a child – or an adult, for that matter – to see in honesty, hear in truth, and accept one's greatness. Let's call that transformational turning point "the instant I first believed." It is never too late to believe in a story and determine, like I did, to make it a starting point for one's own. And it is never too late for an adult to decide to join in on the miraculous adventure of becoming the angel who reflects a child's first glimpse and glory of greatness.

So, here's to the transformational power of the stories in these pages! Here's to the joyful vision of each story touching a million lives! And here's to the expectation that your story will be among those in the next edition!

In faith, love and gratitude,
Susan McLeod
Founding Publisher, EnergyParenting.com

SECTION I: THE FIRST STAND

Energizing Success and Greatness

Energizing success is a key aspect of how the Nurtured Heart Approach goes beyond normal ways of being positive – in heightened, energized and detailed ways that lead a child to begin to truly experience her greatness and her growing ability to enjoy and sustain relationship through successful choices.

The average parent or teacher who has studied conventional methods, even one who greatly values being positive, most often relies on statements like "thank you" and "good job." These kinds of statements certainly convey approval and appreciation to the child and the adult's desire to be supportive and encouraging, but they are both inherently vague and energetically pale. They relay an unclear sense of just why the child is being valued, and they are energetically lackluster, especially compared to the energized responses these same approaches would have us apply when things go wrong.

To have a powerful impact, we need to have powerful ways of alerting our child that his choice, in this moment, not only did not go unnoticed, but that it was strongly valued for the reasons you are clearly expressing right then and there.

These kinds of positive statements have impact because they are given in the context of what is happening in the NOW, in the context of how the child is valued and in the context of how they promote relationship. The power comes from the child being shown that his choice has meaning to the beholder. The power also comes from demonstrating that a great deal of relationship and a great quality of relationship are transpiring in connection with the child's good choice of the moment. Statements like "good job" or "thank you" simply do not provide that level of meaning or that level of relationship or presence.

Taking a stand in this regard is equivalent to refusing to forget that this child's greatness is a flame that continues to need fanning until it is so bright and strong that it can reliably continue of its own accord.

We hope you will see the major importance of and superb results possible from energizing success and greatness as portrayed in the following real-life stories.

Howard Glasser

The Transformation of Patrick

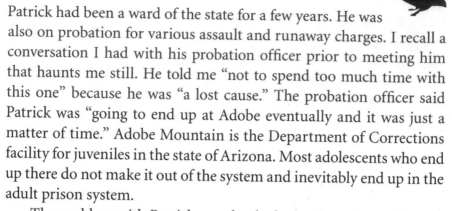

By Lisa Bravo

Patrick had been a ward of the state for a few years. He was also on probation for various assault and runaway charges. I recall a conversation I had with his probation officer prior to meeting him that haunts me still. He told me "not to spend too much time with this one" because he was "a lost cause." The probation officer said Patrick was "going to end up at Adobe eventually and it was just a matter of time." Adobe Mountain is the Department of Corrections facility for juveniles in the state of Arizona. Most adolescents who end up there do not make it out of the system and inevitably end up in the adult prison system.

The problem with Patrick was that he had a short fuse with great aim. He had been in and out of group homes and juvenile detention since age 12 when he hit a CPS [Child Protective Services] worker as she removed him from his home where his schizophrenic mother had attempted suicide. On paper he looked like a 10-foot-tall fire-breathing dragon. He was full of rage and had no significant relationships in his life.

In my experience, these kids ALWAYS respond to the Nurtured Heart Approach because they ache for emotional nutrition. The impact of the approach is two-fold for these children: it nurtures them in an authentic way while providing a first-hand experience of successful interaction. Other forms of behavior management, in my opinion, do not set the stage for success in quite the same way.

My belief was that this angry child was coping in the best way he knew how. Because I saw him as a powerful and intense child who used anger to cope with the tragedy of his life, I was able to see his anger as one of his strengths. My experience with kids who are constantly provoking others into physical fights is that they feel utterly defenseless and powerless. Fighting is a way for them to feel their power. But when they can feel this sort of power in a healthy way, they begin to change in amazing and profound ways. Armed with this wisdom, I dismissed the comments of the probation officer and set my sights on "The Transformation of Patrick."

It was late in the day when I arrived at the boot-camp-style group home where he had been placed by his CPS case manager after being disruptive in yet another group home placement. I was waiting in one of the meeting rooms when my attention was drawn to a disturbance in the hallway. A very tall, slender young man was in the corner surrounded by several staff. He was quite animated. His fists were drawn and ready for action. His eyes were full of panic. He was visibly disturbed, stating that he was "not crazy" and was "not gonna see no !#@*! therapist." I had unknowingly interrupted his recreational time. Realizing this was probably my new client, I approached the conflagration. Patrick dug his heels in deeper, making it clear to all involved that NOBODY could make him do what he did not want to do. I introduced myself in a nonchalant way, was ignored and continued on by apologizing for interrupting his recreation time. I promised that he would be back on the basketball court in 10 short minutes if he so desired. For a moment, he considered my offer.

The staff then tried to run interference, telling me Patrick would not be meeting with me today. He began to escalate again, but stopped himself and said "I'll meet with the lady." He followed me into the meeting room, accompanied by four staff ready for a takedown. Patrick sat rigidly at the edge of a chair and studied me, unsure what to do next. His fists were still by his face, his jaw clenched. I made as much eye contact as he was willing to allow and said, "Wow, I can see that you are REALLY angry but here you are sitting here not hurting anybody, not yelling, not swearing at me. You could be doing ALL those things right now, but you are not. You are being are so strong and powerful in this very moment. How are you able to do it? It's amazing!" Patrick looked at me a bit bewildered, trying to register what had just happened. He then looked me square in the eye and cracked a dazzling smile from ear to ear.

From that moment on, he responded differently when conflict arose. He took a stand and decided he was no longer going to "give away his power." When staff would push him too far or other kids would try to get him involved in a fight, he would tell himself that his power was too important to give up "to a bunch of ignorant fools." He no longer allowed the people around him to decide how he was going to live out his day.

He worked hard to move up in the level system of the camp and quickly attained the highest level. His impulsive lapses in judgment became few and far between. HE became THE example for the other children. For the first time in his life, he made the honor role. At some point in our time together, he began to look at school as an important key to his future. He even began to discuss the possibility of community college.

In a few short months, this young man reached the pinnacle of his transformation! He was able to move back home with his mother and stepfather. He enrolled in high school and got a job to help with the family bills. Patrick learned how to embrace his intensity and share it with those around him in numerous profound ways. Of his own volition, he decided to give back to the camp by writing to the new children "because I know how really hard it is to be there." He had a vision for himself for the first time in his life. Each day he takes steps toward realizing that vision.

Lisa Bravo is a Certified Nurtured Heart Specialist and a nationally recognized speaker on the Nurtured Heart Approach. Lisa is co-author of *Transforming the Difficult Child Workbook* (Glasser, Bowdidge & Bravo, 2007). She is also the founder/director of Parentworx Consulting and maintains a private counseling/parent coaching practice in the Phoenix area.

——————————————————— (♥) ———————————————————

Lisa Bravo's incredible story about Patrick's transformation vividly depicts how one person's courageous attunement to the positive can impact a child for a lifetime. Lisa's brilliant comments simply captured and described the truth of the moment she had with him – a moment that would throw most people off balance. By so truthfully recognizing and acknowledging what was and wasn't happening that was of great value, she completely captured Patrick's greatness in that moment and lit that flame in the core of his being. HNG

In her inspiring story, Lisa exemplifies relentless intention and personal determination to create 'positivity' and resist the professional trap of descending with the weight and limitation imparted through negative labels of a young man on the precipice of prison. She demonstrates the essence of an unflappable core and dramatic healing capacity. In clearly refusing to* *energize negative prophecy imbued by other less inspired professionals, this story shows how a young man's negative spiral can be shifted in dramatic directions and dramatic proportions by a professional holding the ground for a miracle in each moment. JLE*

———————————— ⟨♥⟩ ————————————

*Positivity is a word coined with creative license by Howard Glasser, Tom Grove and Melissa Block (collaborative authors of *The Inner Wealth Initiative: The Nurtured Heart Approach for Educators*). Although not an actual word, it has been invented to convey the positive counterpoint of negativity. Positivity appears in several places in this book to describe the richest, most powerful and delicious sense of being positive!

From Ross the Boss to Zen Truck Master

By Debi Sementelli

I was greeted at my client's door with a big smile and an invitation from her 3-year-old son Ross to "Come and see me!" Little did he know that was my exact mission. I wanted to observe this boy who, by his mother's description, was "High energy! High intensity! Always on the go. Full tilt, no in-between."

The list of challenging behaviors was long: demanding, no self-control, temper tantrums that escalated into uncontrollable fits, and hitting, kicking, and throwing things when angry. These behaviors occurred not only at home but at preschool as well. Routine actions such as eating breakfast and getting dressed were a regular morning battle.

When I first saw her, his mother's body had carried the tired look of defeat. Dad worked long 11-hour days and, in an effort to do his part, struggled to take over in the evening by getting Ross to take a bath and go to bed – tasks not easily accomplished. The stress of having a 'difficult child' was overwhelming for this young couple but they were determined to get help for themselves and the son they adored.

A quote from the Nurtured Heart Approach book came to my mind: "Over-energized children struggle with lack of inhibition. There are times when they cannot conjure up the inner control required to override their impulses to do the inappropriate...often in ways that place them in extreme conflict with their environment or the people close to them."

As I watched Ross playing with his trucks, everything I observed told me this child had an incredible amount of intelligent curiosity and enthusiasm for learning about the world around him. It was clear that energy could barely be contained in his 3-year-old body.

He carefully explained to me what he was doing as he meticulously loaded his dump truck with various toy parts that lay on the floor and 'delivered' them to the 'building site.' He was in that wonderful zone kids get in when they are so totally focused on accomplishing a goal. I felt like I was watching the 'Zen Truck Master.'

Encouraged by what I saw, I decided to try out some things. I started utilizing 'Video Moments' by tracking his actions with enthusiasm. "I see you're working hard to make sure you get all of those things in the dump truck. Now you're moving them over to the dump site and making sure they all get dumped there. I wonder what you'll do next!"

His eyes met mine and there was an instant connection. Perhaps he thought of me as another truck aficionado. I'm not sure, but what was reflected back to me left no doubt: "You get me. And you're affirming me for something that I'm doing that excites me. You now have permission to enter my world."

His mother watched with interest as I continued pulling out more Nurtured Heart video moments. He beamed. When it was time to clean up (a task that was usually a struggle) while I continued the positive recognitions, he happily picked up every last toy and went as far as to make sure to remove something that was preventing the closet door, where all the toys were kept, from closing properly.

While this type of demonstration is not a normal part of my services, sometimes actions speak louder than words. As tired as his mom was, I wanted to give her a taste of how a shift in the way she used her energy could help produce the behavior she was looking for.

It was also an obvious indication to me of how great a fit the Nurtured Heart Approach would be in this situation. We charted our course focusing on trucks as a theme for his credits. Mom used her computer skills to print off a collection of clip art trucks of all kinds. She laminated them at a local copy store and utilized plastic containers for the 'truck dealership' (where they are kept until earned) as well as a 'truck garage' to keep them in. Time-outs were named 'rest stops.'

In addition, I asked her to utilize one of my products, the 'Follow the Animals Routine Chart,' which gives a visual way for kids aged 3 to 6 to keep track of what comes next in their morning and nighttime routines, such as brushing teeth, eating breakfast, getting dressed, etc. The animals are shown demonstrating each step. For young kids, for whom time management is not yet a learned skill, it helps break down tasks into manageable parts. For each animal that Ross followed, he would earn a truck.

While Ross was delighted with the new system, the changes in his world caused him to test it. As the Nurtured Heart Approach warns, "When you get a new roof, you want it to rain!" His tantrums escalated. He shouted at his mother to "stop talking" when she used video moments. I affirmed her insight that he was testing to see if things were really going to be different.

Before, Ross was the boss. He inappropriately bossed his parents and teachers with his behavior. He was not a 'bad boy,' just one of many bright, high-energy kids who come into the world with all four cylinders going full blast and adults who were totally unprepared about how to handle the challenges. None of the 'getting ready for baby' books quite describe this type of child. Parents are just getting used to the idea of having a new person in their lives. Sleep deprivation, new physical demands, changes in the marital relationship, less individual and couple time – all are happening at the same time. Add a child with two to three times the curiosity and energy of other children and before you know it, the child has gained momentum and is pulling you into a vortex of confusion and inadequacy.

But his parents stayed true to the Nurtured Heart Approach. Soon, I was hearing of the successes that were now a regular part of their days. He waited in line for an hour without making a fuss. He and Dad had a great 'Donuts with Dad' day, an item that represented a reward in his credit system. At a church event that was hours long, he was cooperative and calm. He was easier to be around. He stopped hitting and kicking. The list goes on.

On my last visit, Ross' parents looked happy, calm and confident. Yes, Ross still had his moments. But they knew how to handle them instead of exacerbating them. Ross greeted me with that same bright smile that I'd first seen three months earlier. He'd remembered our connection and brought out new toy tools to thrill me with. I happily responded, "Wow! These tools are so cool. I'll bet you can build all kinds of things with these." He beamed and went off to get another item for our impromptu show and tell.

As I said my goodbyes to this now happier family, I reflected on the 'cool tools' that the Nurtured Heart Approach had provided. It's pretty amazing to see what parents can build with them.

Debi Sementelli is a Parent Coach, Certified Positive Discipline Associate and Youth Empowerment Facilitator who has helped parents maintain their sanity while raising capable kids. During the 14 years she's been working with parents and children, her greatest testing ground has always been at her home 'laboratory' in Dallas, Texas, with her two sons, now teenagers.

I love what Debi Sementelli offers us all through this vivid depiction of how she joined forces with this highly energized child. She didn't give 'Ross the Boss' any energy at all, but she displayed the perfect amount of presence with 'The Zen Truck Master' in a manner that led him to perceive a few key things: first and foremost, that he didn't have to go to the trouble of acting out to have her wholehearted involvement and connection; secondly, he recognized that he was being truly 'seen' in a way that translated to being held in esteem, which he further translated as being deeply valued and meaningful.

After testing the approach directly with Ross to assess the level at which he had the optimal response, Debi then took the savvy step of explaining the Nurtured Heart Approach in a way that made sense to Ross' parents and in a format that truly engaged them and gave them a new 'tool box.'

In my clinical work, it has been apparent, time and time again, that role modeling alone is never going to lead to a transformation. My initial interaction with a child is intended to assess his receptivity and the nuances of that receptivity so that I could heighten the message to the parents. This is exactly what Debi did in a most thrilling way. Congratulations Debi and congratulations to Ross and his parents! HNG

Debi's beautiful style of working through a Nurtured Heart window with Ross and his parents gives us all a lesson in how connecting with a child's strengths and interest is the grounded take-off point to guiding a child to her inner greatness and greater things in the world.

Debi is the inspiring guide for Ross' parents to recognize the 'Zen place,' the starting point of honoring and energizing positive terrain through Creative Recognitions and Video Moments. Debi shows us that positioning this take-off point from within the child's world serves as the foundation for the parents to return to again and again as relational guy wires as they guide their child's energy to soar to great heights.

It is absolutely thrilling to see how Ross' parents were prepared to weather all the testing Debi prepared them to expect. After about 15 years as a play therapist, I realized the true magic and gratification of watching as parents step into amazing levels of power as healers with their children. As parents, we sometimes forget the simple power of recognizing and being with our children in their world, in each moment.

This positive, in-the-moment connection with Ross becomes a powerful alliance in support of Ross' greatness as his courageously creative parents sail with new tools of authority, benevolence and focused intention on what they seek to support for their son, rather than fear for him. What a gift for Debi that she was able to assist and witness the highest octave of parents becoming healers and helpers for their son who is now destined for his own greatness! JLE

Kane's Story

By Karen Jennings

Working in a K-4 elementary school, I naturally see a lot of engaging children, but Kane was especially endearing. He had a certain spark and a twinkle in his eye. He was very connected to his family and went out of his way to take care of his little sister once she entered school. He also struggled with a learning disability, which regularly caused him a great deal of frustration. Everyone loved Kane – until he got angry. Kane had a temper that seemed to get worse every year. By third grade, Kane and his outbursts were becoming notorious in our school. He started to lose some friends, and teachers were understandably concerned about his escalating temper.

As the school social worker/behavior consultant, I am called on to deal with students who have behavior issues; Kane had been on my caseload since first grade. Luckily he and I had formed a good relationship, but unfortunately it was not enough to de-escalate Kane's behavior when he became upset.

Kane was the kind of person who had a knee-jerk reaction when he felt something was unfair or unjust; he would immediately go from zero to 60. Nothing could stop him; calm words, reminders, behavior motivators all fell on deaf ears. His face would turn red, his fists would clench and his voice volume would increase exponentially to the size of his audience. Only after pushing a situation to the limit would he muster the ability to slowly come back to a point where he could be reasoned with. By then he would have racked up any number of undesirable consequences, some of which might trigger additional outbursts when attempts were made to enforce them.

Following his tantrums, Kane would always cry and be contrite and apologetic. His standard explanation was "I can't stop! I can't control my temper!" When facing provocation, Kane insisted he was unable to think of any of the strategies he had been taught; he felt as if his temper took control of him. After an incident, he felt bad about himself. His parents were angry with him but also sad that he was having such difficulty at school. I felt rather inadequate and frustrated.

Like all therapists, I was always on the lookout for a new intervention or technique that might work with those 'really difficult' children. So when a flyer for the Nurtured Heart Approach came across my desk, I was immediately intrigued by the title: Transforming the Difficult Child. I took it to the school principal, who looked at me and said "Kane!" I suggested she and I attend a seminar together since we were usually the first to intervene when our 'difficult' students had a problem.

The day we attended the Nurtured Heart training (half way through Kane's third-grade year) was a turning point. As a seasoned therapist, I knew a lot of theories, techniques and methods of behavior modification, but there were a few children who did not respond to anything I tried and sometimes behaved even worse after my attempts at intervention! So it was with these students in mind that I went to the training. What I came away with was not another technique but a new outlook on behavior.

The day after Howard Glasser's presentation, I literally could not wait to get started. I felt energized, enthusiastic, excited and hopeful in a way I had never felt about dealing with behavior problems. As I started finding ways to implement the approach, I realized it was harder than it sounded, mainly because it was a new way of thinking and behaving on my part. Nevertheless, I still had some immediate successes that made me say, "Wow, this really does work!" Our principal told me she was having similar results.

I had a few weeks to get accustomed to using the Nurtured Heart Approach before Kane put it to the test. As was very common, the triggering incident occurred on the playground during recess. The call came into the office: Kane was having a meltdown over some perceived injustice on the playground and was refusing to follow the direction of his teacher, which was to go to the office. As I walked onto the playground, Kane spotted me and immediately began yelling that he was not going inside with me. He threw his coat on the ground and began running into the field away from school. I made the decision not to chase him (I knew from past experience if left alone he would come in with his class when recess was over) and went back into the school to watch from a window. As his class began to line up to come inside, Kane joined them as if nothing had happened.

As Kane came down the hall, he spotted me standing outside his classroom. He stopped and angrily told me he was not going to the office and no one was going to be able to make him. "I want to congratulate you!" I said. He looked at me like I had lost my mind and asked "What for?" "For lining up and coming inside with your class. I know you are really mad and you didn't want to come in, but you did. You have finally got control over your temper!" I went on, "I can't wait to call your parents and tell them what we have been working on all this time has finally happened!" By this time Kane was pretty much in shock so he put up minimal resistance when I told him we needed to go to my office to figure out the consequences for his earlier behavior.

As we talked about what had happened, I could see the emotions shifting across his face: his smile in response to the praise he was receiving for controlling himself and being able to talk about the incident, alternating with his anger and struggle to remain in control. I continued with statements like, "I can see you are so mad and want to yell, but look at you!! You are sitting here using a calm voice, talking about what happened, hearing your consequences, it's so great to see this!!!" These seemed to really make it impossible for him to lose control. In the end we called his parents and, after quelling their fears that he really was in trouble again, made a huge deal out of Kane finally being able to control his temper. He was then sent to the office to do his time-out (which he did without a peep) and returned to class, where he finished the day without further incident. The message we sent and he heard was, "Yes, you messed up, but you accepted the consequences, didn't make it into a bigger problem, and it's over. You are doing it!" An opportunity for success was created.

In the past, Kane would have continued refusing to follow adult direction, his parents would have been called in for a meeting, he might have earned an in-school suspension for the next day, and he would have ended up in trouble at home. Instead, we started Kane down the road to feeling successful. His parents praised him when he got home and he felt great about himself. The next time he had a problem, we reinforced his ability to regain control even though he had initially lost his temper. From then on his outbursts became much less frequent and very short-lived when they did occur. He became capable of doing consequences without incident and his fourth-grade year went very smoothly.

Now we routinely use the Nurtured Heart Approach every day in many of our classrooms. Teachers often stop me in the hall or come by my office to share a Nurtured Heart story. We continue to meet as a group so we can support one another and celebrate successes. Our goal is to have our entire school district using the Nurtured Heart Approach.

Karen Jennings is a Licensed Clinical Social Worker who has been in the social work field for 28 years and the Maine school district for the past seven years. She is now a Certified Nurtured Heart Specialist. In addition to the Nurtured Heart Approach, Karen also uses animal-assisted therapy in her practice, bringing her therapy dog, Nemo, to school every day.

I absolutely love Karen's relentless inspiration and her deep caring for Kane. It could have been Kane 'mutiny' just as easily because so many professionals call it quits when encounters with kids like this not only continue to be fruitless, but when the cumulative effect feels like a burnout. I also love that, despite her vast experience, she was willing to take a fresh look at an entirely different viewpoint. It's so easy to become attached to methods, even methods that are not quite working, and lose that sense of openness.

The best part of the story for me is that, after just learning the approach one day, the very next day she masterfully converted a challenging scenario into an experience of success! And she did it in a way that Kane was able to discern being celebrated for his great decision and in a way that he was able to recognize that he still had to fulfill his consequence. And talk about masterful, in that very first day she is already connecting the dots by helping Kane's parents get on board with appreciative responses.

How wonderful that Karen is fostering constructive collaboration in her school and holding a vision for her district. There will always be children entering schools who are at risk to have a horrendous time and at risk to create horrendous scenarios for the adults in the building. Teacher attrition is at an all-time high in part for this very reason. The average cost to a district is

$14,000 for every teacher quitting or moving to another school. However, when teachers discover powerful methods that are effective, they are much more likely to stay put. We now know schools that have zero teacher attrition! Congratulations to Karen, her principal and her colleagues!! **HNG**

What a blessing to have such a powerful angel as Karen in this small and committed school district! It is heartening to know she is one of so many committed to work on the front lines with children like Kane. Instead of another child lost to negativity in a problem-focused system, another life ring has been powerfully offered. It is deep support with the highest, most far-reaching, lifetime fortitude imaginable. In this courageous school, another young man has been given a new belief in himself and his abilities! **JLE**

The Mother I Want to Be

By Lisa Bravo

I write to you this evening after receiving a song of appreciation and hand-drawn pictures from my two amazing, energetic and kind children ages 10 and almost 8. Today was a typical day with my 'Nurtured Heart' children.

I picked them up from school curbside as I always do. Danielle, my almost-8-year-old, saved half of her snack for her brother and presented it to him in a carefully wrapped napkin. Christopher, my 10-year-old, hugged his sister and then his mother. He handed Danielle a bag of Cheetos that he traded for at lunch because he "knows they are her favorite." He openly tells me about his day, about his "fantastic behavior" and "great attitude." He asks me to turn down the radio because he really wants to get his homework finished before we get home. When I ask him why, he says because he wants to have enough time to work on an 'MD' project (MD stands for Mother's Day) and play outside for a bit. And so the day goes on – most of the time very much like this.

When I think back to the way I parented before I stumbled upon the Nurtured Heart Approach, I remember a conflicted and stressed-out parent who was completely out of gas. As a therapist for the past 15 years, I have always worked with families and children. I tried to stay abreast of what was being offered in terms of therapy and parenting information. I had been a parenting instructor and worked with hundreds of children by the time I had my own. I figured it would be a piece of cake. Little did I know how unprepared I was.

From the beginning, I realized things were not going to follow along as all those parenting books had promised. From the moment Christopher was born, he was active and strong-willed both as a baby and toddler. Naps were rare if at all, and he constantly demanded to be held. When Danielle came along, his neediness manifested itself in acts of aggression, usually toward other children. Needless to say, playgroups were few and far between. Very few people understood his intensity or how to handle it. I tried several different parenting approaches; most would work for a few days or weeks, and then there would be a big blow up. Almost always, my husband and I would throw our hands up and do more of the same – more of the same that was not working.

To make matters worse, his sister turned out to be 'textbook perfect' developmentally. She was very social, very sweet and very compliant. She also had severe asthma as a baby and toddler, so she consumed a lot of our attention and nurturing. Christopher quickly learned that the only way to feel part of our family constellation, the only way to 'get more,' was to be an adversary. And he was very good at it! It pains me to admit that I would silently rejoice when he was sick with a cold or virus because that meant I would get a break from this energy-zapping little boy of mine.

I felt ashamed that I, a therapist, could not manage the behaviors of my own child! I used all the tools I had and, if any improvement resulted, it usually did not last. While browsing through a bookstore one day, I saw Howard Glasser's and Jennifer Easley's book *Transforming the Difficult Child: The Nurtured Heart Approach*. I leafed through it, thinking it was in line with what I already believed about children and how they live in the world. It was not until several years later that I began to utilize the approach in my home.

When Christopher reached kindergarten age, we enrolled him in a small private school that was big on discipline and structure; we figured the more structure, the better his behavior would be, right? WRONG! As the year progressed, Christopher became increasingly anxious and resistant about going to school. Each morning he would cry and carry on, saying he did not want to go. Each morning I encouraged him and sent him on his way telling myself this is what he needs. (Not to mention, I secretly enjoyed the break I got while he was gone.)

Parent-teacher conferences were nothing less than a traumatic experience. Christopher's anxiety increased to the point where he had begun to bite holes in all of his shirts. His hands were also peppered with scabs because he had begun to bite them. He had no fingernails left to speak of because he had bitten them down to the quick. Right before my eyes, I felt like my worst nightmare was being realized. It all came to a head when I had the final conference with Christopher's kindergarten teacher. She said she was concerned about his 'hyperactivity' and 'distractibility' in the classroom and he "would probably benefit from a visit to a doctor to see what is going on with him." She went on to say that she believed he might have ADHD and might benefit from medication.

It was in this moment that I took a stand. I decided that no matter what, my son would not be defined in this way. I had worked with children for a long time and I knew he met criteria for many of the behavior traits of ADHD, but I somehow intuitively knew that there was another answer for my son.

I set out to find a different school and I started to really research different parenting theories. Not long after, I had the opportunity to see Howard Glasser give a presentation about his work. Although I was very impressed and very inspired by the beauty and reverence of this approach, I was still very skeptical. I did not believe that the dramatic results he spoke of were even possible. I happened to be in a position at work in which I needed to model parenting skills for parents in a community mental health setting. I was always of the belief that if I wanted other parents to try it, I needed to give it a try at home.

I went home that night and started my experiment. I began with Active Recognitions and creating successful moments while I began to set the table. Danielle immediately responded. Eventually, so did Christopher. Gone were my arguing, fussy, whining children. It was pure magic!

Within a week or two, my son was well on his way to transformation. Today he is a kind, nurturing, energetic little being that revels in his own goodness. We still have a meltdown from time to time, but they are few and far between. Christopher catches himself before he gets to the point of no return – he puts himself in time-out and is back in the game in the blink of an eye.

It has been years since he has chewed holes in his shirts, and nail clipping is now a regular event at our house. He loves school and the adventure of learning something new. He is confident and encouraging to other children and adults. He has a fearlessness about him that is hard to articulate.

In the last year, he and his sister, along with the other children in our neighborhood, formed a group to 'do good deeds.' They wanted to "have fun helping people with their friends." Their 'gang' has even been interviewed by the local newspaper. They have developed inner wealth, just as the authors of the Nurtured Heart book describe therein.

The Nurtured Heart Approach began as a way for me to simply improve my relationship with my son. It has evolved into a lifestyle change that has affected every aspect of how I live in the world today. Inwardly, I am profoundly changed. Outwardly, I am a confident, kind and happy mother. I AM the mother I always wanted to be!

I am exceedingly fortunate to know this therapist and these two incredibly transformed children. I did not know Christopher when he was adversarial but I experience him now as an amazing young man who manifests his intensity and greatness in a myriad of ways that are deeply caring, thoughtful and wise. He is so receptive to statements of appreciation and in turn is so appreciative and loving toward others. He is an absolute pleasure to be around, and I believe he will continue to evolve the ways he manifests his greatness. Once a child is comfortable in his skin with his particular blend of greatness, he will continue to polish the splendor of who he is.

And Danielle is another amazing being. The statements of wisdom that come out of this child's mouth are astounding. She's the one who stops everyone in their tracks with the profound level of choice and judgment she exercises in how she negotiates life and situations. She could run a highly effective and highly meaningful humanitarian program or organization now as a middle school student. That's how powerful she is. Power in the best possible way.

And her mother leads the league in positive power. She gets her power by 'remembering' to be in that powerful place of appreciativeness and by remembering to point the gratefulness in her heart to ways her children are being successful in her eyes. But letting her heart tell the truth is the real point of power. And this great mother and therapist has refined it to an art form. HNG

This heart-rich story brings such deep resonance and remembrance for me – both as a children's therapist who also wasn't prepared for the maelstrom of parenting an intense child, and as a mother of an intense child saved by this heart-driven healing.

It takes deep courage as a professional to realize that the standard skills and experience are not enough with certain children. It takes equally great power as a parent to acknowledge when power needs to be shifted. This mother offers a lesson for those of us who have had to let go of conventional perspectives in our parenting journey. If we are lucky, we have powerful and courageous children like Christopher and Danielle to bring us to these amazing changes! JLE

Mike's Story

By Jan Hunter

When teen-aged Mike rejoined our family in 2004, he'd been living with his biological mother for three years. He was angry at the world, failing most of his classes and, although of sophomore age, still a freshman in ranking. He was refusing to study or do homework. He was setting himself up to fail and just didn't care. Any suggestions to do otherwise were always met with anger and an adamant refusal to budge from his stance that his way was right – even if he failed.

In the beginning of this journey, I really think he was looking to be noticed for anything good. So we started there, Video Moments to the hilt! "Mike, I see that you are starting your homework....Wow, Mike! You have all your homework done early tonight. That shows organization and dedication to your goals!...Mike, you are showing excellent study skills. I see that you're keeping good notes from class and are using them to study for the upcoming test....Thanks for letting us know that you've signed up for Encore. That's a wonderful tool to use and take advantage of the extra tutoring that's available. It takes lots of courage to say 'I need more help.' It also shows lots of maturity on your part to accept the extra help as well."

He balked at first, letting us know he knew what we were up to. That was okay, we were happy he remembered from years previous and summer visits with us. But as things progressed and he continued to thrive with the recognitions, we saw his confidence grow amazingly. He was excited to share report cards, biweekly progress reports and conversations he was having with his teachers.

I was also making sure that his teachers and counselors were on board with the Nurtured Heart Approach, and it paid off big time! I initiated e-mail contact with each teacher at the beginning of each term. I asked for bi-weekly updates; all they would have to do was give me Mike's current status in the class and one positive interaction from that time period. One teacher even asked Mike to be the contributor and choose the interaction he wanted to share. Mike came home that day very excited to share what the teacher said, and I think that's when the transformation really began and his own inner wealth took over. We shared each of these e-mails with Mike when he arrived home from school. There were times he beamed as he read the e-mails, and once he mentioned how good they made him feel, especially after a really discouraging day in a class. His teachers were really noticing him for his accomplishments and efforts.

During his junior year in high school, Mike worked so diligently and magnificently that, by earning all of his credits, he was a full-fledged senior the following fall (2005) without having to take a single summer school class!

As I went with Mike to senior enrollment for the fall, I have to admit I was a little shocked at what I saw and heard. As we walked toward the table and the assigned teacher, a smile and light gathered in her eyes. She was thrilled to see him! She was excited to share his enthusiasm for her class and the work. She didn't even have to reach into her grade book to pull out his grades to make the report to us. As she looked at his list of 'hoped for' classes, she was impressed to see his choices, as was I.

Mike, who had always struggled with math and balked at having to take anything beyond the basic required classes, now listed Algebra II as his first math class of choice instead of the easier class. His reasoning was he would need it for future college-level drafting, art and science classes. Applause, applause! He even added chemistry as his final science class. More applause! He still needed a signature on his math class selection and, as he headed to his current math teacher for approval, the Algebra II teacher stopped him and said he'd already heard how well Mike was doing and would sign without looking at his grades! How cool was that?!

His art classes would also contribute to his homework load, but he felt sufficiently confident now to handle it. He was experiencing so much success right now in the classroom, at home and in his scouting program. For us, this was a significant change. His recent desire to succeed in the classroom has bred lots of recognition in varied directions.

The guidance counselor even made a point to come from the opposite side of the room to congratulate him on his class choices and the tremendous leaps in grades as well. She made a point of bragging about him not only to me, but to the teachers at surrounding tables... he was beaming and nearly dancing down the hall as we left.

I'm still shocked at the difference from one year ago! Helping him return from a totally angry and frustrated point to wanting to do his best has really been a challenge for our whole family, but one well worth it. The Nurtured Heart Approach truly played a significant part in this change. Mike has always marched to a different drumbeat, and now we openly applaud him as he makes all the right choices to his own beat! Even today!

Update: Mike did walk across the stage with his peers and graduated with the class of 2006! We were very proud, but he was the proudest! He had to work so very hard. Algebra II and Chemistry were nearly his undoing for a time. Because of the academic challenges, Mike also made the decision to attend extra tutoring before and after school and do as much extra credit as possible to keep his head afloat in one of the classes. This was a big step for Mike. He was having to admit that he needed extra help and couldn't do it solo. What an incredible acknowledgment. And his willingness to share that with us was a leap for him. He now realized that the choices he was making were GREAT choices! It was now his choice to study, work harder than he'd ever done before and openly look at his own successes, large and small. He was internalizing what we'd known all along and shared with him daily; he now had complete ownership in his 'transformation.'

Jan Hunter is the Mom of seven children. Her primary focus and occupation is M.O.M. (Masters in Motherhood, Mentoring and Motivation). She is a Certified Nurtured Heart Specialist and helps parents and schools in Oklahoma implement the approach.

———————————————— ✍ ————————————————

What a heartening story of cultivating greatness and inner wealth! Jan began with baby steps of acknowledgment. This reflection to Mike – the wisdom of his basic choices and Jan's deep faith in him – roots itself in an inner reserve and resilience that Mike carries today.

I love how Jan provoked the positive flow that came for Mike in his high school setting after she involved his teachers and school counselor in the approach! This flow of school 'positivity' seemed to provide a cascade effect of acknowledgement of Mike and his efforts. This is a lovely testimony to how greatness recognized and reflected in our homes and schools becomes greatness internalized! Mike is now a young man making powerful personal and career path choices on his own behalf, and Jan has taken her path of nurturing greatness beyond her family to our global community! *JLE*

To me, Mike's story is really Jan's story. How utterly painful it must be to feel walled off and helpless in the face of your child's anger, frustration and indifference. It would be so easy to go into a tailspin and feel "why bother" or "how could this child be so ungrateful" or a million other reactive takes on the situation.

But Jan had a plan and she was unwavering and totally dedicated, courageous and powerful in living out that plan. How else could she have not thrown in the towel? This woman relentlessly chose to see only success and create even more success in the face of this child's determination to be oppositional. And somehow her determination and viewpoint transmitted to this young man that he was truly valued and truly meaningful in this woman's eyes. And somehow, some way, this transmission made its way to Mike's heart in a way that helped him value himself and see his own life as meaningful. In my eyes, both Jan and Mike are the heroes of this story. Just as he could have given up in a million and one ways, Jan could have done the same, too.

I love that Jan got every last significant person on board. As a dear friend of Jan's, I can totally picture her doing this with such dignity and purpose – and such results. Mike's success was not an accident. It was purely a function of Jan's choice to confront him with who he really is – underneath all of who he used to think he was – a stunning person of greatness, not just any greatness, but intense and wonderful greatness. I am so glad he now gets to experience his passion for life and the fruits of all his hard work. What fun! He so deserves to savor the successes. *HNG*

Strong Enough to Stop: Taking Inner Wealth to a Greater Level

By Gabrielli LaChiara

I was contacted by a mother who felt she needed some counseling regarding her use of the Nurtured Heart Approach with her 8-year-old son Sammy. He had informally been diagnosed with OCD (Obsessive Compulsive Disorder). Among many other behaviors that this mother was upset and struggling with was her son's constant pulling of his eyelashes. She and her husband had tried many parenting approaches that had worked temporarily but none had lasted.

After using the Nurtured Heart Approach for three weeks, she had seen significant changes in her son's oppositional behaviors. She was pleased with his ability to take direction and specifically to take 'no' for an answer. She was effectively resetting her son. Though happy with the results, she was still concerned about his eyelash pulling and wondered if it was evidence of a deep, chronic anxiety problem or a sign that he was truly unhappy. I instructed her to apply the approach much more intensely. She began energizing her son relentlessly for his self-control, his great choices, and specifically his impulse control. She found every way she could to create a portfolio of success for her son in these areas. Sometimes she would even call it 'self-control' when he was just sitting in the car with his seat belt buckled, an activity that he never had any problem with!

After about six weeks of continuing progress, I suggested that she try something completely new. Since there was ample evidence of her son's impulse/self-control and his ability to take 'no' for an answer, he was effectively re-setting and loved his newfound power. With new confidence in her son, she announced to him one day, out of the blue, that he was ready to stop pulling his eyelashes. She recounted numerous situations where he had proved he was capable, for example by stopping himself from arguing, by taking 'no' for an answer despite his strong feelings, and by using his power to accept limits and carry out his consequences. The next time he pulled his eyelashes, she simply said 'reset' and reminded him with clarity that he doesn't do that anymore. To her surprise, he stopped. With pride, he beamed at his own success. They rejoiced in his pride and his own newfound sense of self.

For this child and I believe for many others, OCD is connected to a negative portfolio. Once emotional safety in the family was established and this child's portfolio of success was built up, he was able, with ease, to stop his compulsion. Three years later he has no signs of OCD.

Gabrielli LaChiara is a Certified Nurtured Heart Specialist who has been working with families and children for 20 years as a trained group facilitator and family counselor. She is co-founder of MotherWoman, Inc., and is the northeast region's leading expert on the Nurtured Heart Approach. Gabrielli's practice, ClearLight Counseling, is dedicated to helping people cultivate inner strength, increase consciousness and develop tools and resources for personal growth and success.

Gabrielli's amazing story of transformation offers us an inspiring glimpse at what happens when a mother is encouraged through wise counsel to 'go deeper' into the success portfolio. By building a convincing bridge of evidence for her son, she shows him that he has the power and ability to manage his anxiety behaviors.

Not only is this a lovely example of not energizing the negativity of a compulsive behavior, it also reflects how a reset can be used energetically and non-punitively. How many children might be off medication for this defined disorder if the parents created such a powerful portfolio and focused only their positive lens in response to behaviors that merit change?

Thank you Gabrielli for your wise words, essentially a call to other parents to provide similar benevolent support and change for their children! Bravo to this mother and son as well for walking the bridge of empowerment and self-control so bravely and relentlessly. This is the heart of true healing! JLE

It was truly difficult for me to decide which aspect of this story most merited highlighting. Certainly it is a great story about not energizing negativity, because most parents could have gone headlong into accidentally giving tons of energy and relationship to the negative behaviors. And certainly it is a great story about a nuanced way that resets can be used where most adults, even most professionals in the mental health field, wouldn't dream of giving a consequence to a physical manifestation such as pulling eyelashes.

However, for me, it truly is a story that speaks volumes about how far we can go with the adventure of positivity. In my practice, this was most often the defining piece that made things happen. I felt that my greatest therapeutic power was in fostering that next level of positivity that would finally awaken some child to the call of greatness within his soul. I found over and over again that there were always greater levels of positivity to be discovered and created.

Gabrielli inspired that in this mother and trusted her instincts to take it still further. Congratulations to all involved. HNG

From Boot-Camp Bound to Heaven on Earth

By Michelle Baxter

There are six in our family: me, my husband David, our 13-year-old son Mitchell, our 6-year-old daughter Emma, our sweet little boy Devon who passed away when he was just 6 weeks old and our yellow lab Scooter. (How could I forget our lizard Billy, so I guess there are seven of us.) Dave and I often referred to our house as the Baxter Zoo and often he would answer the phone with that reference.

Our story begins when our son Mitchell was in first grade and his teacher told us that we needed to medicate him or she was going to put him in a privacy desk with barriers all around him. Devastated and irate, as you can imagine, we started a long journey of testing.

Medication was the solution that was recommended over and over again. After a couple years of behavior that we were unable to manage and several visits to school, we gave in to the professionals. We tried medication after medication with Mitchell, each having a multitude of side effects ranging from loss of weight to physical outbursts.

By the time Mitchell turned 12, we were at a complete loss on where to go; doctors were insisting that our son needed to be sent to a boot camp or things were only going to get worse. We thought, "How can things get worse?" We were already dealing with physical outbursts that sent each of us to urgent care as well as broken doors and holes in walls. In a desperate search to find something else, I happened upon the website for 'Transforming the Difficult Child' and was intrigued to say the least.

We had tried several other approaches (from '123 Magic' to 'Love and Logic') and read a ton of books, but nothing was successful for more than a week or so. Dave and I decided that we had nothing to lose; as it turned out, we had everything to gain.

Because of our lack of success with many other approaches/theories, I decided I wanted some guidance along the way. So we hired a family coach who was certified in the Nurtured Heart Approach. I feverishly read the book and started implementation of Step One – Active Recognition (Kodak Moments).

We spent the following week pointing out everything we could possibly come up with from "I noticed you're wearing a red shirt today" to "I see you woke up easily" to "You look frustrated." Mitchell tells us now that he thought we had lost our minds but he says he was enjoying the newfound attention.

During this time I was in disbelief. I thought: "They have to be kidding me that this is going to help." But sure enough after a week we saw a tremendous shift in how Mitchell was interacting with us and how he was channeling his energy in positive ways. He had been notorious for swearing and physical outbursts. Now, because we were noticing and verbalizing to him what we had once considered insignificant things, he was choosing not to swear, and the physical outbursts decreased, all because he was being energized for doing everyday things.

At one point, I remember him playing on the computer and, as I checked on him, he began to argue with me regarding something he wanted. Ordinarily I would have engaged in the negativity, but I remembered that in that moment I had a choice to make. I looked at him and said, "I see you are really frustrated" and walked away. First, I couldn't believe I had just done that; and second, I couldn't believe that I didn't hear another word. Wow, could this really be working? If only it will stand the test of time.

On we went to Step Two, Experiential Recognition, Step Three, Proactive Recognition, and Step Four, Creative Recognition, introducing each in small doable ways over the next few weeks. These steps involved adding our values, re-framing our house rules and shifting the way we were making requests to foster more successes. I wasn't sure how we were going to accomplish these new steps and still be successful. I started with adding our values to the comments we were already making, like "Wow, I totally appreciate you being responsible waiting with your sister after school" and "You're being successful right now choosing to not argue with your sister."

Next came the rules, and we began pointing out successes like "I really appreciate that you have not sworn this morning; thanks for following the rules." Or "You're really using your power in a positive way by not arguing with your sister. Awesome job following the rules."

We were getting the hang of it. Coming up with successes was becoming second nature and we could not believe how extremely easy this was. He was already being successful in so many ways, all we had to do was acknowledge and reinforce them so he could see his own successes.

Step Four just flowed for us after realizing that we had inadvertently been giving him choices all along. We quickly switched to "I need you to take your shower right now" instead of "Will you please go take your shower?" It was amazing; off he went without a complaint and on we went pointing out how successful he was: "I really appreciate you taking your shower when you were told to and following directions so well."

Mitchell was changing with every new step and the proof for us was when he came home one day very upset. I pointed out right away that he seemed very upset ("I notice that you look very upset"), and the next thing I knew he was opening up, telling me that some kids he had been hanging around with were going to skip school the next day and do drugs. (Wow, I had no idea that 7th graders would be faced with these pressures.) He continued on, explaining to me that these were not the type of kids he should be hanging out with, and right then and there he chose to go his own direction. "Awesome job Mitchell, doesn't it feel powerful to be able to make such positive choices?" Could this really be happening, we kept asking each other?

This all sounds amazing, but don't get too excited; remember our daughter Emma who was five at the time. Up until this point, she had not given us any problems and her behavior was typical for a five-year-old. We implemented the approach with both of them at the same time, and to our surprise she was the one testing us now.

She began throwing tantrums, screaming and antagonizing Mitchell. We realized that she had always been the one who received the positive attention and now her older brother was in the spotlight. We had some work to do! We amped up the energizing for both of them and within a week her behavior was not only back to normal but had actually improved. She was leaving her brother alone and success continued.

Soon it was time to introduce Mitchell and Emma to the next phase of the approach, following rules and completing chores and responsibilities. "I've noticed how both of you have been making such good choices that I would like to give you credit for those choices and reward you." I went on to explain the idea of the credit system. The first words I heard were: "I have to earn points for privileges that I already have?" I pointed out how successful they were being and told them it was their choice to participate, and they will earn points for following the rules, practicing positive behaviors and completing chores. "Until you decide to participate, all privileges will be on hold, but remember you will still be earning points."

Much to our surprise, they were both willing to participate. It was a bit of touch and go with Mitchell debating for points, but in the end the process has been extremely effective. Our children were following the rules, practicing positive behaviors and even helping around the house as well as taking personal responsibility for themselves. Pretty amazing, since in the past we couldn't even get Mitchell to brush his teeth or Emma to brush her hair, not to mention having previously tried every behavior chart imaginable with no luck.

Soon it was time for consequences, and I was mortified at the thought. There is no way that these kids are going to take a time-out, or 'freeze' as we refer to it in our house, without major meltdowns. I introduced the concept one afternoon by saying that I know I can't stop them from breaking a rule, but from now on when a rule is broken, I will be administering a freeze, which will need to be done immediately without conversation or debate. I further explained that these time-outs were very different than those that both children had come to hate so much (a minute for every year old they were and off to their bedrooms); these would be shorter in duration and would take place wherever they were. Within an hour, I had to exact a freeze from both for breaking our no arguing rule. To my surprise, both children froze immediately with no complaints, not even a peep. Okay, really, whose house is this and whose children are these?

Since there were only a couple weeks of school left, we decided to tie the school successes directly to home rather then involving teachers at this point of the school year. Mitchell already had a daily planner used as a communication tool between school and home. I decided to award points based on the information provided by teachers: up to 40 points for a good day, 30 if he had only a late assignment, 15 for only a negative comment and 5 if he received both a late assignment note and a negative comment about his behavior.

Notes on negative classroom behavior have ceased and late assignments have been reduced. I don't even have to cover this point much anymore because he will say, "I had a late assignment; I only earned 30 points today."

To prepare for the upcoming year, I provided the book *The Inner Wealth Initiative* to his case manager and gave his prospective teachers some documents I created through the process. I have offered my assistance to develop a plan that will work for all of us, especially Mitchell.

This is where our story ends for now. We are patiently waiting for our meeting with all of his teachers and are excited at the prospect of having a positive new school year.

We have had our speed bumps and I anticipate many more to come, but now we have the tools to be effective in positive ways. We can't say enough about this approach after working with it. The approach has helped us create a calmer home environment where everyone gets along, and Dave and I are excited to come home and spend quality time with our children. It is an amazing transformation. It is a wonderful sight to see our children laughing and smiling again! We have become a much closer and happier family thanks to this approach!

Remember, you always have another choice in the next moment!!

After such a positive experience, Michelle Baxter and her husband Dave decided to attend the Advanced Training and now are both Certified Nurtured Heart Specialists who assist others families with challenging children. They reside in Columbus, Wisconsin.

——————————————— ☙ ———————————————

This is the kind of story that I read in awe. I am so impressed by the level of dedication Michelle and Dave needed to conjure up the desire not only to give new approaches one more try, but to do so having experienced so many failures. They stayed so clear and purposeful and moved through the recommended strategies in such an organized way. They stayed so calm in the face of anticipated and real challenges and were able to get quickly to a point of being very creative with their recognitions. It warms my heart to see they could finally trust that they could effectively communicate the love they had all along through the vehicle of this approach. They now have a structure for the way they form the words their hearts want to say in a way that their children can really hear.

Maybe the biggest point to be made here is that they are the true heroes of the story. They are the ones who took the advice and ran with it. They could have read the book and lamented that it wasn't worth the effort or nixed moving forward for a thousand different reasons, considering all they had been through. But they didn't let anything stop them. In the face of fighting the push for boot camp and more medications, they did what it took and it was this effort that made the day. And fortunately, by their emerging heroics, Mitchell and Emma both get to be heroes as well! **HNG**

Bravo to Michelle and Dave for the courage to shift their family's experience and lifestyle in such joyous and far-reaching ways. Michelle's sweet story really takes us through the universally felt emotions of so many parents and the deep gratitude they experience when things start to shift. This happens when parents take an unflappable stand for their children's honor and righteousness. **JLE**

—————————— ☺ ——————————

Inventing Yoga Jacks

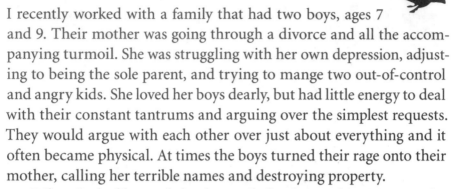

By Lisa Bravo

I recently worked with a family that had two boys, ages 7 and 9. Their mother was going through a divorce and all the accompanying turmoil. She was struggling with her own depression, adjusting to being the sole parent, and trying to mange two out-of-control and angry kids. She loved her boys dearly, but had little energy to deal with their constant tantrums and arguing over the simplest requests. They would argue with each other over just about everything and it often became physical. At times the boys turned their rage onto their mother, calling her terrible names and destroying property.

When I asked her to define her goals for the coaching process, she became very resolute. She said she wanted her children to get along without fighting constantly and wanted to have a better relationship with them and enjoy being with them. Smiling, she added that she would love for them "to be able to play a game, any game, as a family, without fighting or tears." She had been implementing the first phase of the Nurtured Heart Approach with some success. Even though her boys would cover their ears and say, "Stop being so nice, it's annoying me," she would stand firm in her relentless pursuit of the positive.

At our fourth in-home coaching session, I had the opportunity to witness the transformation that had taken place. The mother opened the door and said, "I forgot you were coming; you are just in time, follow me." She explained to me that just moments earlier her younger son, Evan, was chasing Grant, the older one, around the backyard with a mallet. Grant then stopped in his tracks and announced, "I'm not doing this!" She praised the boy for his courage and bravery and power in stopping himself from fighting back. Moments later Evan came in (the mallet outside) and announced he needed to 'reset' upstairs. The mother gave him a few moments and then went upstairs to energize him for taking a time-out on his own. Peace had prevailed!

The children then asked me to join them in playing a new game they invented. The boys took out a set of jacks and two sheets of paper printed with common yoga poses. They explained, in unison, how to play the game. They said that we would each take turns and, if we picked up a jack, we got to pick a pose. Everyone would then have to do the pose that was chosen. Part of the game, they explained, was to see "how many times we can encourage another person."

They decided I would begin the game because I was their guest. We each took a turn as the children consistently cheered for the one whose turn it was. They told me that cooperating in this way was fun because they got to try the newest pose. As each pose grew in complexity, so did our laughter. When I say we laughed, I do not mean your everyday run-of-the-mill laughter. We laughed so hard our bellies were aching. It was pure joy! There was no dialogue about who was first or who was winning or losing. There were no sermons, no lectures, no pleading. I looked over at their mother who was thoroughly engulfed in the game. She was emanating her pure love in that moment. She was not only enjoying her boys, she was IN JOY with them!

When I pointed this out to her later, she told me that she now realizes how depressed she had been and that she needed to take care of her own wounds in order to fully 'be' with her children. Her insight and brilliance inspire and astound me to this day.

What an amazing tribute to this understandably overwhelmed mother who took the steps she needed to make this great transformation happen DESPITE HER DEPRESSION. I think the hard work she undertook to help her children was very closely aligned with the self-healing work she felt she achieved for herself. In fact, it is my opinion that what came first and made the space and the impetus for this mother to feel she healed herself was the gratitude she chose to show her children. Being grateful for what I perceive in others and seeing the greatness in others has always created further inspiration for me to do the same internally.

I absolutely love the inspiration Lisa provided this mother, the joy and creativity this family was now experiencing, and the enjoyment Lisa was able to take in what she had set in motion. HNG

Lisa's story is a sparkling example of the amazing shifts that can occur when an even overwhelmed parent sets a powerful intention to create new energy and experiences for her family. I believe this mother's clear intention to have less conflict in the family and truly enjoy her boys not only set this energy in motion, it became the torch for the whole family's healing.

Lisa shows us the real alchemy of supporting and nourishing this mother's healing intent for her family. She offers the mother workable tools to really 'be' with and energize her boys in ways they need. They are powerful tools that enable this mother to withstand the boys' initial resistance to being recognized for strengths and support as a forerunner to offering a new level of positives. This powerful trail guides the boys to the inner strength they need to energize their own greatness and that of others.

The master game-playing boys are now empowered enough to create a new game – one that moves them all to realms of greater possibilities and boundless joy! Bravo to Ms. Bravo and to this courageous family! JLE

The Rubber Chicken of Responsibility

By Tammy Small

Johnny was a boy who had struggled in school since he was a kindergartener. You could see the smile in the yearbooks slowly fade from 'taking on the world' to being weighed down by it. To him, in 8th grade, what he was in store for was just another 'parent/teacher conference' where everyone cared more than he did. Before Johnny's arrival at the conference, I worked on shifting the focus of the parents and teachers from Johnny's errant ways to his gifts. We were now ready to give Johnny our full Nurtured Heart Approach (albeit a modified version of untrained but best intentioned parents and teachers). His social studies teacher went to get him.

Johnny sauntered into the principal's office like a man on a mission ("Get this over, so I can get outta here," his smirk implied). Eight adults gathered to nurture his heart and see if we could find the key to Johnny's engagement. We faced one adolescent well armored from years of skill at 'getting it all wrong.'

"You can use this chair or the principal's." (She was not there, but we were using her space to corral the child into compliance.) "Take the principal's," I encourage. "Sure," Johnny says as he sits down and slides the chair up to the conference table like a professional C.E.O. "I am glad you could make the time to meet today," he says, breaking the ice in a way that no adult could. One of the great things about Johnny is that he was funny. Everyone knew he was funny – but he had hidden it for so long, only attempting mumbled jokes or small asides to his most trusted, truant friends. He lacked the confidence to be the clown. More importantly, he lacked the confidence to step into his greatness.

"Keep going, Johnny," I say, chuckling with the others. "You are on a roll. Tell us why you have brought us together." He bites on this game – and sits taller in his cushy leather chair of authority. "Well, we are here today to discuss me, and how to get me to do my work." The adults are laughing, relieved to be free of those first words. "And what should we do, Johnny?" I lean in, nodding and smiling. And so it begins. After he did his spiel, we all went around and told Johnny what was great about him: what he is doing well, where he is giving his best and so on. Then we asked Johnny what was great about himself. For many kids, you can do this first, but for kids who are depressed and so far from acknowledgment of their greatness, having others recount what they see is a huge springboard to their success.

Letting Johnny be Johnny and giving him energy for this was, in and of itself, a huge gift for him. We then gave him ideas of how he could translate his successes – his good qualities – into classroom successes. Then we asked him for ideas of how to improve in Social Studies class. "Well, I could ask more questions when I am lost." He was incredible as 'Principal' Johnny...and as struggling adolescent Johnny, coming to a difficult table but being fully present, fully honest. I tell him so. I ask him for more. "If I could just keep track of my notebook..." Teachers agree and the English teacher says, "What if we were to tie a rubber chicken to your notebook? It would be hard to lose then, right?" He smiles and nods and we know he is hooked again. Be unique – but be responsible.

"Would this be Johnny-ish enough for you?" I ask, matching Johnny's direct eye contact across the table. He confirms the absolute silliness and seriousness at the same time. "I think it would work," he says, smiling imperceptibly. The Rubber Chicken is just one of many plans that are made that session, but I am compelled to see it through.

That afternoon, after feeling well-nurtured by simply nurturing the greatness of Johnny (merely hidden behind bad habits), I find it – Johnny's rubber chicken, that is – at the counter of a drug store. It was not the small key chain version, nor the larger type used by magicians, but a more perfect seven inches of quality rubber – candy included. I guess it was ready for a child's Easter basket. And for me, it symbolized Johnny's own Easter revival.

At the end of my typically challenging day, I grab my bag, and the Rubber Chicken (R.C.) pokes its head out. It reminds me that I have one more thing to do. Recklessly, I sneak into the classroom of 8th graders engaged in Writer's Workshop and poke Johnny on his shoulder, beckoning him to follow me, R.C. tucked conspiratorially under my jacket. We sneak around the corner and I produce R.C., all 7 inches of genuine rubber and boasting some non-descript candy that comes out of his mouth. With hushed gravity, I explain "You have to be very

58

mature to handle this chicken." We are both smiling at the banality of this statement. But I continue, "You must attach him to your notebook, but then resist this." I squeeze R.C.'s belly and produce the 'quick to make enemies of teachers here to help you' sound. We both stifle a giggle. He tilts his head back, his smile so genuine, no sweat of anxiety. I mean business and neither of us misses the oxymoron of a serious rubber chicken. "Should I wait and help you attach it tomorrow, or do you have the notebook?" Can you handle it now is my implied question. And he gets it. "I'll take care of it" he says, taking the chicken without even a test squeeze. "Best of luck," I say to his back, as he nods with a smile and tucks the rather large Rubber Chicken of Responsibility into his pocket. I am still chuckling as I head down the hall toward my car, not a squeak to be heard from the classroom.

Tammy Small has been an educator for 24 years, initially as a junior high teacher and then as a high school counselor after earning her Master's Degree. Desperate for the unpredictable adolescent, she returned to junior high and younger grades, serving as a counselor in a private K-8 school in Washington. Tammy created and coordinated a peer mediator program (with 5th-8th graders) that won a Washington State Golden Apple Award in 2005. Her passion for 'GREATIFYING' kids (the term she uses in her own school) grows as she trains local school personnel and families.

_____ (S) _____

Tammy's zany approach in the cultivation of greatness is ripe with creativity. Not only did she provide a transformation of energy for Johnny, she expanded the vision of many educators. Tammy shows us unconventional means of sustaining relationship, meeting a child where he/she is, and using theatrical humor as a means of providing tributaries of success and motivation. JI.F

I love how Tammy has deepened her own personal style to fit her personality and how this intention of GREATIFYING those she has contact with allows her to bring her special evolution of the Nurtured Heart Approach forward. I hope she finds GREATIFYING very gratifying. And knowing Tammy, I am certain there are so many 'Johnnys' benefiting from her influence in the many schools in which she trains and consults. HNG

_____ (S) _____

The Worthiness Creed

By Ellen Thomas with Susan Zola

I was asked to pop in to visit the 6th graders on their first day and say a little about ISS (that's 'In-School Suspension' at most schools, 'In-School Successes' at ours). As I walked down the hall, I thought: I can't say ISS is a BAD place, that's too negative. But I don't want it to seem that it's a day spa, either. I don't want to give a whole litany on the rules and why kids NEED to follow the rules. So I thought, what is it that they didn't 'get' from last year? What one thing could I tell them? I didn't even have it ready until I took the microphone. Here's the message I came up with:

"I honor each of you for how quietly you walked down the hall.
You are SO WORTHY of the respect that you show others!
You are SO WORTHY of your ideas, and knowing when to share them, and knowing to wait patiently.
You are SO WORTHY OF RECOGNITION!
YOU ARE WORTHY OF YOUR SUCCESS!"

I started using that verbiage daily and found it works. It always works. A student the other day didn't want to go to class. I say, "You are worthy of your contribution to that class." He is still wandering mentally. "You are so worthy of showcasing your maturity and leadership as an important part of that class!" He's coming back now. "You are so VERY worthy of your teacher's time! Do you know that when you are not there, there is a gaping hole where your integrity is supposed to be? You are so definitely worthy of being where you can be recognized for your amazing mind." And he opened the door and took his worthy self right on in there!

At another time, I used the same strategy with two kids getting too touchy with each other, not fighting, just very tactile. "You are so worthy of keeping your hands to yourself." Boom, done. And then I went on, "Look at how quickly you embraced your worthiness!"

Many educators are still 'rule oriented.' Call it what you want: expectations, rules, it's all the same thing. And adults seem to love the sport of reminding kids about the rules. Instead, I created the

"Worthiness Creed" for lack of a better phrase. It has all the rules embedded in it. Now, I can remind all I want. I can remind them of how worthy they are of whatever it is that's expected. At Jefferson Middle School, everyone is WORTHY!

I am worthy of respecting others as I want to be respected.

I am worthy of remaining alert and attentive.

I am worthy of listening to others.

I am worthy of waiting patiently to be recognized for my ideas.

I am worthy of dedicated productivity.

I am worthy of showing attention to detail.

I am worthy of being able to remain calm in the face of conflict.

I am worthy of other people's time.

I am worthy of recognition for my talents.

I am worthy of integrity.

I am worthy of honesty.

I am worthy of your care, and showing care to others.

I am worthy of my individuality.

I AM WORTHY!

Ellen Thomas is an educator at Jefferson Middle School in Champaign, Illinois. She oversees the In-School Success (formerly 'Suspension') program. Ellen's life philosophy deeply reflects Nurtured Heart tenets. When asked her philosophy of education during her interview for the teaching position at Jefferson, Ellen responded: "Everyone wants to be a part of something, to be heard, noticed, cared for, acknowledged. Everyone wants to feel like they have something to contribute."

Jefferson Middle School principal Susan Zola offers the following eye-opening facts about her school and the impact of the Nurtured Heart Approach:

Jefferson serves over 700 sixth, seventh and eighth grade students in a diverse middle school in central Illinois. Demographic data show that minority students comprise 47.5 % of the school population, 19% of students receive special education support and almost 40% are eligible for free and reduced lunch. Jefferson began implementing the Nurtured Heart Approach in the fall of 2006. All staff were trained and many worked closely with Tom Grove, Nurtured Heart Approach consultant, to refine their skills. Tom is co-author of *The Inner Wealth Initiative: The Nurtured Heart Approach for Educators.*

Within one year, Jefferson saw a 16% overall decrease in discipline referrals, while discipline referrals of African American students decreased 20%. The staff continues to discuss the power in pursuing the positive. They are all now acutely aware of how the words and actions of adults can propel students to great heights or catapult them to places of despair. The school's early results using the approach are quite promising. Both quantitative and qualitative data speak to the power of the Nurtured Heart Approach and its potential impact on both the adults and students within a school community.

Dr. Susan Zola is a trainer in implementing the Nurtured Heart Approach and has served as a classroom teacher, elementary and middle school principal, and assistant superintendent for curriculum and instruction. She firmly believes that educators have the capacity to transform students by the power of their voices. She believes that building the 'inner wealth' of both adults and students is a key to transforming the work conducted in today's schools. She was a contributor to *The Inner Wealth Initiative: The Nurtured Heart Approach for Educators* (Glasser, Grove and Block, 2007).

Ellen walks her talk in such a profoundly relentless and empowered way; her energy and call for positive movement are palpable. A super-fired style of Creative Recognition, her 'Creed of Worthiness' shines her commitment to energizing esteem and honorability while calling forth (exhorting) the spirit of presence, integrity and perseverance. Ellen's creed becomes a beacon to light the path for those students and educators at Jefferson School lucky enough to receive the wisdom of two professionals so committed to seeing and cultivating greatness in our schools. JLE

I honestly did not at first know what to make of Ellen's interpretation of the Nurtured Heart Approach. But then I realized that she is simply applauding a child's heart and soul in her very own idiosyncratic way. Because the fact is that there's no single way to use this approach, and it is absolutely best used in a person's very own way. I am grateful to Ellen for illustrating this so brilliantly. She has the courage to be strong in herself and her interpretations and convictions, a message that she conveys to the students as well.

I have always thought of my Kodak Moments and Polaroid Moments as ways of snapping an instant and then relaying to the child what it was that I saw relevant to meaningful choices and actions. Ellen simply invented another kind of photographic device that indeed captures a moment ahead of the current moment in which she is simply telling the truth of the worthiness she sees in that moment.

Congratulations to Ellen, to Dr. Zola (who has orchestrated great change in a school that was barreling down the road in the opposite direction), and to all the others who have successfully lent wise and helping hands to the efforts at Jefferson Middle School. Everyone there is really making the transformation to greatness happen. HNG

Karen's Story

By Kathryn B. Sherrod, Ph.D.

While working at a state psychiatric hospital for adolescents, I met many adolescents who had learned all the wrong things. They had learned that they were stupid, ugly and a bother to the world. Before arriving there, I assumed I would find it depressing to work with such troubled teens. I was wrong. I had no idea how much I would come to love the kids, the staff and the place.

Who could love a state psychiatric hospital? Aren't they under-staffed, unattractive and exhausting? Well, yes. Ours was. We never had enough staff. The buildings were old and desperately needed to be renovated. There was always more work to be done. So what was there to love? The way kids changed while they lived at the hospital! One adolescent in particular stands out in my mind.

Karen had first tried to kill herself when she was seven years old by hanging herself. She failed. She failed at getting along with her parents. She failed at getting along with teachers. Eventually, she was put into special schools to try to control her behavior. That failed. She got worse. She was put into a series of residential placements in an effort to change her behavior. That failed. She got worse. She quit eating much of the time and got very thin. Despite being thin, she got into some impressive fights, showing unexpected strength.

Finally, Karen was admitted to the state psychiatric hospital. Initially, she failed in our place, too. She lost too much weight and had to be placed in a medical hospital. When she was released, she cut herself when no one was looking and had to be readmitted to the medical hospital. Despite one staff person assigned full-time to watch her so she would not cut herself, she still did so and was back in the medical hospital yet again. When she was discharged, two full-time staff people were assigned to watch her. (That means that, for each of three eight-hour shifts, two people watched this one adolescent to keep her from hurting herself because one person per shift wasn't enough to keep her safe.)

After three months of Karen having two people devoted to her 24 hours a day, she started getting better in response to persistent positive comments by staff. She initially shrugged her shoulders when she was given positive attention. Nonetheless, she seemed a bit more receptive to comments about her intelligence than about anything else, so we stuck with what worked. Line staff, who often get a bad reputation, spent hours with Karen paying attention to her and encouraging her. (I know they gave her a lot of pep talks along with the Nurtured Heart recognitions, but nobody's perfect.) I made it a point to always compliment staff on their dedication to all the students, not just to Karen. We wanted these kids to do well, and many felt our positive intent for them, even if we stumbled at times.

As a therapist, I felt I was working with the tiniest increments of positivity. On days Karen ate, I told her I could see how well she was taking care of herself by eating instead of starving herself. On days she didn't eat, I led our conversations in other directions. I was even applauding her when she wasn't cutting herself. Finally, Karen started looking around instead of down. She started talking instead of ignoring people.

Staff now could see more opportunities to encourage Karen because Karen had more positives to recognize. She got to leave the dormitory to go to the fenced grassy area for cookouts. She smiled and I told her she had a lovely smile. Then I told Karen she needed to start observing herself and complimenting herself. She didn't want to do that, saying it was too hard. It seemed impossible to her. I asked her to practice by saying out loud some of the things she liked about me and saying why she liked them. That was hard, but possible. I asked her to tell staff members what she appreciated about them and specifically what they had done and were doing that she liked. Slowly, with practice on other people, she became willing to verbalize nice things about herself that were observations of what she was doing in the moment.

Karen started wanting to live instead of wanting to die. Her staff assignment was reduced from two to one. She did well. Then her one-to-one status was discontinued and she became a regular student, sharing staff with everyone else. She continued to do well. I asked her one day what was different now. She said, "In all those other places, they tried to catch me screwing up and I knew sooner or later I'd screw up so there wasn't any point in trying to do anything better.

Here, you seem to want me to do well and you point out when I'm doing well. When I screw up you punish me and then let it go. I always have another chance." (At this point, she looked at the floor before looking back up again.) "You keep wanting me to do well and giving me another chance because maybe you care about me." (She looked down again, apparently feeling too vulnerable.) I was stunned to hear a 16-year-old be so communicative and appreciative. I told her how proud I was of her for feeling so deeply, for observing her world so clearly, and for being willing to share with me. As she finally allowed herself to feel the nurture she was being offered, her heart and mind healed.

About 18 months after being discharged from the hospital to a foster care home, Karen called to tell me she was in her final year of high school and only had a few months to go. She said there were two other foster kids in the home who were "...okay sometimes, but who got on her nerves sometimes." She had a part-time job after school, had friends, and was already accepted into the Air Force following graduation. She reminded me that one of the field trips our staff took her on was to the local airport. She said she had never been to an airport before that field trip. On that day she decided she wanted to fly.

Karen never lost her dream and now she was going to live her dream. I was amazed that she had called and asked her how she found my phone number. Turns out she had kept my business card all that time. A teenager who keeps up with anything that small for that long is a miracle! I was also amazed by all her good news. There's no stopping a teen who wants to live!

Kathryn B. Sherrod, Ph.D., is a psychologist who utilizes Nurtured Heart concepts in her private practice in Nashville, TN. She has a 14-year history teaching graduate psychology at Fisk and Vanderbilt Universities and worked with children and adolescents from 1988 to 2004 in an inpatient psychiatric unit. Kathryn co-authored a book entitled Infancy, published in 1978 – the first book in a Life-Span Development series. She also published a book on the 12 steps for "Christians Distressed By Imperfections (Theirs or Others')."

I love the relentless pursuit of the positive in this story. Kathryn clearly had to inspire and re-inspire the hospital staff to keep going in this pursuit despite all the obstacles, despite the myriad ways and reasons they could have thrown in the towel. It is because of Kathryn's heroic role at the hospital that the staff could ultimately experience their own heroism of contributing to Karen's transformation and enable her to be a hero. Every person touched by this remarkable turnaround now knows irrefutably that, if it can happen with this girl so determined to end her life, it can happen with anyone. I wouldn't be surprised if many more children at the hospital benefited from this great intention of positivity.

The point is that, once a person is wrapped in the experience of this new way of conducting oneself, it is hard to turn back. Even people peripheral to the process are profoundly affected. Congratulations to Kathryn for her remarkable work and to Karen for her remarkable turnaround. **HNG**

Bravo to Kathryn for courageously bringing this paradigm into a mental health hospital setting! Her relentlessness not only likely saved a life, it supported an institutional shift – offering a nurturing, healing structure in a setting often associated with horrifically negative conditions for both staff and patients.

It is deeply touching to read of Karen's gradual bloom through painful layers of healing – taking in and discovering lovable and indomitable parts of her psyche through Kathryn's recognitions of Karen's positive steps and refusal to be hooked by negatives. For Karen to ultimately choose a career in flying speaks to the depth of her experiencing new wings and power at a critical core level. **JLE**

Waking Up to the Gift of Positive Lectures

By Gabrielli LaChiara

Waking up was always one of the most difficult times of the day for my son. As a baby, he would wake up crying and colicky and I would need to immediately nurse him, which was only sometimes successful at stopping his crying. As a toddler, he woke up screaming, even from naps. Somewhere around age 3 he began waking up with an alarming "MOM" screeched at the top of his lungs, followed with some type of demand such as "I need water!" or "I'm hungry!" or "Lay down with me!" or simply "I need you!" I began to dread morning.

His piercing scream would jolt me awake like a fire alarm. After the initial jolt, my placating would begin. Whether it was nursing in his infancy or later walking, holding, bouncing, baths, outdoor walks at 5 a.m. or car rides – whatever it took, I continued to go through these gyrations to meet this child's needs. I would bring him his demanded object (me, water, food, etc.) only to go through 10 or 15 minutes more of demanding, crying and screaming behaviors.

After reading the book Transforming the Difficult Child, I had new excitement for relating with my son, who by now was age 7. I understood so clearly that what he was screaming for was ME. Now this was something I could always give and even have some control over.

I started by super-energizing him at bedtime, which made our bedtime routine even more meaningful. We had always loved bedtime but now I understood that filling him with specific evidence was the key to creating real change and fulfilling his deepest needs. Instead of engaging in my customary long and intense conversations about his disrespectful behavior, I began every day by telling him how 'respectful' or 'loving' he was. I would find three or four instances during the day when he made choices that I saw as respectful and tell him so. I also told him how mornings could be: we could wake up happy, loving and excited to share our day.

Although mornings got a bit easier, he still awoke with a scream and demands. However, within a week, these episodes lasted no more than 10 minutes. I could quickly energize him and his demands would stop. This, I thought, was amazing success. I was so proud of both of us. Then the unexpected happened. One morning I heard him rustling in the bed and braced myself for the 'morning alarm.' Suddenly I felt a small arm on my back, soft and gentle, his voice softly singing "Good morning my sweet little mama." My heart melted with love. How much more beautiful can it be than this?

This heart-warming story touched very close to home for me, the mother of an occasionally hard to console son. Gabrielli shares openly an anguishing subject that few parents speak of but usually experience one time or another. How do we handle and support the energy of a distressed, yet inconsolable, child without giving fuel to neediness or reinforcing helplessness?

This mother's relentless perseverance to stay present, patient and available to her very needy son during his first 6-plus years is admirable in and of itself. But the real miracle here was how she shifted her attention from responding to neediness to proactive fortification. Her new use of 'positive talks' (versus those negatively reinforcing lectures on disrespect) was code for building self-esteem and providing essential emotional fill-ups during the day. It takes a powerful, committed mother to encourage and transform a powerful son. JLE

This story brings tears to my eyes and opens my heart. It brings out the emotions every one of us can feel when a child finally is fully 'found' and finally can come out. What a great example of bringing forth a much better version of a bedtime lecture. IING

To Your Greatness with Admiration for Your Journey

By Shelah Schenkel

The personal success I found with the Nurtured Heart Approach was during and after an advanced certification training conducted by Howard Glasser. I had utilized the approach for several years prior to this training. However, the advanced training brought the Nurtured Heart Approach to my heart in addition to my cognitive center. It allowed me to 'feel my greatness' and take it to a higher level. Knowing is one thing. But feeling it is completely different. It was a profound experience that everyone should be capable of having at least once in their lifetime.

The greatness of a person became a concrete concept instead of an abstraction during this training. Afterward, I began using this new 'greatness' not only with clients, colleagues, friends, and family, but on MYSELF as well. The manner in which I recognized negative thoughts and transformed them allowed me to have positive feelings and feelings of greatness internally. I found myself talking about my greatness in my head, feeling immense gratitude for life and my experiences.

I began changing negative thoughts by integrating techniques of the approach into my daily thought processes for myself instead of eliciting external guidance. I terminated the negative schemata and replaced it with a new joyous one. Additionally, I utilized positive Active Recognitions and made sure that deep inside I was recognizing my greatness.

At first it felt funny. I almost felt conceited, or like I did not deserve to spend this much time having positive thoughts about myself. In the advanced training, it felt nice hearing others say great things about me, but it was very difficult for me to do it for myself. I feel our society dwells on negativity while instilling low self-concepts.

Consequently, for me, it was complex at first. Keeping in mind that it was a complicated concept for me to allow myself to believe I was GREAT, with practice and consistency I reached a point where I not only am comfortable in my own skin, but expect myself to treat me well. I can recognize my greatness as a person as well as the greatness of my spirit. Nurtured Heart put value on aspects of my personality as opposed to finding fault. I give credit to Nurtured Heart for awakening a new spirit within me that is infinite.

Shelah possesses a Master's Degree in clinical psychology and is a Licensed Professional Counselor in Missouri. She is a certified trainer of the Nurtured Heart Approach and uses the approach to help foster children and their biological families reunify and maintain a stable, warm, loving environment. Shelah is a member of the Association of Comprehensive Energy Psychology (ACEP) and uses a combination of Energy Psychology and Nurtured Heart Approach in working with her clients and promoting intense family cohesiveness.

––––––––––––––––––––––––––––– ⟲ –––––––––––––––––––––––––

Shelah's deeply personal sharing gifts us in many essential and heartfelt ways. Her story highlights a commonly invisible, yet deeply destructive, emotional epidemic – that of inner violence and the ways we diminish both our power and happiness through negative self-thoughts and judgments. She gives beautiful and powerful voice as a healer healing herself, who is then so much more able to bring her healing gifts to those she helps in the world because she, too, is walking the path of inner healing and greatness. JLE

I am so grateful to Shelah for sharing her inner experience with this approach. This story is the perfect icing on the cake to this section on Energizing Success. It's really all about two things: Taking an internal stand on refusing to accidentally energize negativity and taking the ultimate stand of fiercely remembering to energize success and greatness in oneself.

Shelah's journey to greatness is very parallel to my own experience. I simply became intrigued with experimenting with using the Nurtured Heart Approach internally and felt determined, once I tasted how powerful it was, to barrel down that road with tenacity. I had a clear sense of knowing that the gift of all this would be a tremendous internal shift to being positive in a core way, almost like changing default settings on a computer. In my case, this was from my pre-existing default of negativity to a new one of greatness.

I should back up a bit. In trying to push the limits of how far this could go, I practiced on myself, beginning with internal thoughts of appreciation and recognition, as in the Nurtured Heart Approach. Then at some point it dawned on me that there was another higher order road to take. Subsequently I began finding ways to see and cultivate my inner sense of greatness. Try that internally for even a few weeks and you will see amazing changes to every facet of your life.

After seven years of doing this internally, I decided it was time to share this process. I did so for the first time at the 2007 Advanced Training. And it was there that Shelah was first exposed to this notion. It is truly amazing to me that just a matter of months later she attained the level of confidence and mastery she describes in this great story. She obviously exhibited wonderful determination and clarity of purpose. Those are truly qualities of greatness.

I contend that her particular blend of qualities of greatness was there within her and there for the taking all the time. However, it is truly a matter of recognizing and claiming it. She is so correct that it can feel so odd at first. It did for me and it still does now and then, but at the same time it becomes increasingly real and increasingly wonderful to really stand and walk in greatness. I hope you choose to experiment in this way as well. The great and fun thing is that there seem to always be new and never-ending levels to explore. Blessings!! HNG

SECTION II: THE SECOND STAND

Refusing to Energizing Negativity

Taking a stand to refuse to energize negativity can be tremendously challenging. It is so easy to fall into the trap of accidentally giving the gift of words, time, emotions, presence, connection, intimacy and relationship when things start going wrong.

The vast majority of advice in the world of parenting and classroom management will lead you to respond in the midst of a problem unfolding. If you follow any of the countless books, magazine articles, or even popular TV advice shows on the subject, you might well be inclined to discuss challenging issues as they emerge or to react with strong admonishments or harsh pronouncements in response to problems. However, even open-minded attempts to mediate issues and differences, explore feelings, or compassionately give warnings can be the metaphoric equivalent to 'the $100 bill' worth of energy and relationship that a child perceives he is receiving in exchange for creating a moment of adversity.

There were times while parenting my own daughter when I delivered what I thought to be positive little pep talks, and she looked at me and stated, "Dad, you're not using your method!" Yes, I was giving a pep talk, and I did convince myself that it sounded positive, but it was occurring in the midst of a contentious moment. So I really wasn't walking the talk of refusing to energize negativity, and then and there I realized that 'leaking negativity,' as my colleague Tom Grove likes to say, can be amazingly subtle.

Even subtle leaks of negativity can be counterproductive, especially for a child who already has the impression that energy and relationship for success are hard to come by and for a child who is steeped in myriad first-hand experiences that confirm to him that people respond in more alive ways to adversity. For these children, it is crucial for adults to find creative ways to refuse to energize negativity in order for the child to form a new portfolio of success.

The child absolutely needs to see that there is no longer connection available in relation to poor choices. That, along with the other two stands of the Nurtured Heart Approach, is what makes the transformation come to life.

Here are some stories that demonstrate the resolve and clarity one needs, both traits of greatness, to stand in the decision to not energize negativity.

Howard Glasser

Go Out and Make a Difference

By Susan Redford

The beginning of this most miraculous odyssey came when I attended my first Nurtured Heart workshop in Sacramento in September 2005. I was so ready to get out of the helping profession. After 14 years of counseling, it occurred to me none of us were helping; in fact we were often contributing to what I referred to as the 'revolving door.' The client rotates in, connects with the therapist over problem after problem and eventually rotates out through the revolving door – only to realize that the valued relationship is gone. Therefore, more problems are created, and back through the revolving door the client comes. The only time the relationship can be activated is through problems. I didn't ever think it was a conscious process on the part of the client or me as the therapist. It just was. I was tired, exhausted, burnt out and ready to look for a mindless job. Flipping burgers came to mind; I could be an amazing Whopper-flopper!

When a flyer arrived for the Nurtured Heart training, my inclination was to pitch it into the trash. Then something amazing happened....I swear it 'called' to me. I retrieved the flyer and registered. A week or so later as I entered the training, I was surprised to see two of my colleagues there as well. By the end of the training, I knew I had found the missing link for which I had so diligently searched in my career.

A week later, I happened to attend another training, called Seeking Safety (created by Lisa Najavits, Harvard University), an evidence-based treatment for individuals with co-occurring trauma and substance abuse problems. This curriculum-based treatment deals with building a foundation of safety as a first treatment protocol for the combined issues of trauma and substance abuse. I could certainly see the value of this type of curriculum with our clients.

At the time, I was working with the Child Protective Services (CPS) Social Services unit assessing and treating people, most of whom had become involved with the CPS system because of crystal methamphetamine (and/or other drug) use, which had cascaded into the customary neglect and/or abuse issues often associated with the use of substances. In the county in which I worked, crystal methamphetamine use was occurring in almost epidemic proportions (and not surprisingly, throughout the United States).

So, somewhere amongst the two trainings, light bulbs began going on in my head. I could see the value of the Seeking Safety curriculum, but it was simply a curriculum. In my career, I have seen curriculums come and go, particularly in the substance abuse treatment field. The typical substance treatment approach always seemed to stick in my throat. As a dually licensed mental health and substance abuse professional, I could never understand why the rules for treating substance abusers were dramatically different than those for people with mental health problems. While there seemed to be a genuine positive regard for mental health clients, the opposite was portrayed toward substance abusers. I consistently observed a confrontational, get-in-your-face, stereotyping, accusatorial kind of approach (once an addict always an addict...hello my name is _____ and I am an alcoholic, addict, etc.). It never made any sense to me.

Throughout my career I worked with and referred individuals to these types of programs. For months prior to my Nurtured Heart Approach/Seeking Safety trainings, I had battled internally with the horror stories my clients shared regarding their experiences in these programs. I was literally beside myself trying to figure out how to best transform what appeared to be a system of abusing people in the name of treatment.

I was fortunate to be working with a gifted and incredible colleague, a substance abuse intervention counselor with years of experience in a variety of treatment settings in several states. At the time, the county in which I worked seemed to be slightly behind the substance abuse/mental health co-occurring treatment curveball. The two fields co-existed as separate entities (and often collided as a result of the dramatically different paradigms/approaches) – unlike many other states that had the foresight to combine the treatments based on what the research indicates is a stronger, more effective protocol. At any rate, I was supremely blessed to be able to work with this wonderfully intuitive colleague.

After we had both attended the Seeking Safety training, we decided to form a women's treatment group that applied the two trainings. We submitted a proposal to our CPS supervisor and Mental Health supervisor – what visionaries! They gave us the green light and within the week, we were off and running. I was insistent that our Seeking Safety group only be implemented using the Nurtured Heart Approach as an overlay to the curriculum.

We simply were not prepared for the results. I was clumsy using the Nurtured Heart Approach, but I was relentless in the pursuit! Three months into the group, we were having great results; the women were coming and participating. Then I made the trip to Tucson, Arizona, and completed the week-long Nurtured Heart intensive training. It was a life/career/heart-transforming experience. As I walked into our first group after the intensive training, my co-facilitator said to me, "Susan, something is different about you. What is it?" I told her we would do nothing but the Nurtured Heart Approach in our group on this day. "But I haven't had the training," she replied. "Don't worry," I said, "You are a natural. Follow my lead." And follow she did. Thus began the transformation.

&

In our group on that day was Sophie, a 19-year-old mother of two young children with a history of crystal methamphetamine dating back to the age of 13. She had a history of 'failed' treatment episodes (as the substance abuse folks were so fond of recognizing), including a 30-day residential treatment program and a long-term women's intensive outpatient program. She was in jeopardy of having her children detained if she could not successfully complete her CPS case plan – which included both substance abuse and mental health treatments. She could never seem to follow through with her scheduled mental health sessions. She was good about scheduling but had multiple no-shows documented. And despite the consequences, she continued showing occasional positive drug screens (for crystal methamphetamine).

On this day, Sophie checked into group expressing her anger and frustration at living in a 'hell hole' of an apartment loaded with black mold that was making her children ill. She had been to the doctor multiple times with her children, had been calling her landlord repeatedly without any resolution, had no income and was unable to find other suitable housing on her Section Eight grant. It began to dawn on me that this woman was a miracle just waiting to happen.

I turned to her and said "Right now, I have to accuse you of being a good mother. Everything you have told us so far tells me that you are a good mother. You have taken your children to the doctor, you are giving them their medicine, you continue to clean your apartment, you are calling the landlord, and you are looking for new housing. I know because I am a good mother and you are doing everything I can think of that a good mother might or could do to make a difference for her children. I just have to accuse you of being a good mother." The silence was stunning. In a moment, the young woman's hands came to her face and she leaned forward and began rocking in her chair as she began crying. "Nobody has ever accused me of being a good mother. They just get in my face and yell at me and tell me what a rotten mother I am, that I am no good because I used drugs, and then they tell me I can never be a good mother." Now there are no dry eyes in the group.

About one month after this particular group session, this young woman announced she had found clean, adequate housing for her children. Her CPS case was successfully closed. I have not seen her since. I think she is out there being a good mother.

❧

There is another story to tell, about a very large woman with such intense energy and such pride in her 18 to 20 felonies for assaults. She was fond of saying "I get near [this person or that person] and I just break out in handcuffs!" She gave anger and rage a totally new meaning. Well-known to the CPS system, Betty was a mother of two who epitomized every stereotype of a truck driver, which happened to be her chosen profession.

Betty had previously been involved in a lengthy go around with CPS, her children having been detained for child abuse and neglect secondary to crystal methamphetamine addiction. After her first CPS case, she had at least four years of sobriety after a year in substance abuse residential treatment and another year in intensive outpatient treatment. She was fluent in the AA/NA lingo with years of involvement under her belt. Talking with her was like having a conversation with the Big Book; rarely, if ever, was there a real conversation with the authentic, wonderful human being she is. Most people were just terrified of her, including her CPS Social Worker. She would call the Social Worker and make the most outrageous demands, expecting that they would be met "or else." And here she was now, stepping back through the revolving door of 'the system.'

When she was referred to me, Betty was in a 30-day substance abuse residential treatment program following a lengthy relapse and the subsequent detention of her children. We had been in a number of sessions up to this point. Sometimes, being in session with this extremely powerful woman was a combination of appreciating her brilliance while feeling as if I was in the midst of a rodeo trying to rope in an untamed, charging bull. Still, she was responding magnificently to our group process based on the Nurtured Heart Approach.

Then came my opening. She had been discussing her anger at this person or that person or this system or that system and mentioned an incident the night before with her almost 18-year-old son. "I don't know what happened, but we just had a conversation. I didn't feel like being angry at him, so we just talked." My reply: "Right now I have to accuse you of being a really gentle person, Betty. You have given us the irrefutable evidence of that today. And when I think about it, you have given us the evidence of being a gentle person all along. You are respectful in group; you listen to others and give them very wise feedback; you share your wisdom with others in such a gentle way, and you are an incredibly wise woman." As she sat there in the silence following the compliment, a strange look came over her face, as if we could see the information landing in a very different place inside of her.

Next, her face was covered with her hands, she began rocking, and we witnessed her capitulation into her own goodness. "I remember when I was a gentle soul; it was before the sexual abuse. I just started being hard and mean to keep myself safe. Right now, I just remembered what it was like to be gentle again." From that moment on, the transformation cascaded. Interestingly, both my co-facilitator and I noticed another facet of the transformation. Betty's vocabulary was no longer steeped in 'recovery' lingo; rather, it was truly a reflection of her inner intellect and true self.

Incredibly, what we also began to notice was a system transformation as well. First the transformation from the inside out in the client, then the client approaching her Social Worker in a Nurtured Heart way, and finally the Social Worker transforming her reaction to and interaction with the client.

The day after Betty was accused of being a gentle person, I got a call from her CPS Social Worker. "Susan, I just have to ask you, what have you done with my client?!! This morning she left me a message and this is what she said: 'I need to ask you if you can do something for me. It is not urgent. I know you are busy, so only get to it when it is convenient for you.'" The Social Worker told me she had never heard the gentleness of tone in this woman's messages before.

In the year since this happened, the gentleness continues, and I still have social services and mental health workers commenting on the transformation of this most courageous, feisty and delightful woman. (By the way, she has been clean for over one and one-half years as of this writing.)

And I guess that would have been miracle enough, but it is not the end of the story. About two months after Betty graduated from the Seeking Safety/Nurtured Heart group and her CPS case had been successfully closed, she came back to group. She was tearful as she disclosed she had just learned that her daughter had been sexually molested and had finally felt safe enough to tell her mom the secret. Betty went on to say her daughter was terrified of losing both her parents – her father because he was sure to be killed (once this mom found out), and the mother because she was sure to go to jail for killing the father.

This wonderfully transformed woman continued on her course of gentle understanding. She walked her daughter through the legal system, and despite her own similar childhood abuse, found the inner strength, reserves and inner wealth that enabled her to help her daughter heal.

☙

Another woman in our group, Tessa, was so timid – almost afraid of her own shadow. On the day she was attending her first session, we were using our Nurtured Heart focus and Tessa said, "Susan, I just wish you could be my shadow and you could come home with me and keep complimenting me like you are right now." Another seasoned group member reflected back, "Oh honey, stick with us for one month and you will be comfortable with your own shadow." The day after she started group, Tessa's CPS case was dismissed. But rather than walk away from services, she stayed in group. On the day she 'graduated' from the group, she offered this advice to the members: "I don't know when it happened, but something opened up inside of me. I was no longer afraid. I was okay with me. Stay here. It will happen for you, I don't know when, I just know that it will."

I am amazed at the transformation of entire systems as a result of using the Nurtured Heart Approach. Among our clients in the group, we regularly hear compliments one client to another such as, "You are so peaceful today. I just want to sit close to you."…"You have grown so much since you started group. You have such wisdom." The approach then filters to the social workers and mental health workers from the women. No one can interact in quite the same way with the client or with each other when they have been touched by this approach. In my experience, we all began to settle into our own authentic skin and bones and began to have wonderfully meaningful collaborative processes and interactions. The CPS unit in which I worked was transformed into one of the most desirable work environments I have ever experienced.

My co-facilitator and I are relentless in appreciating the barriers faced by and the strengths of each woman. We acknowledge what a miracle it is for a woman to merely show up for group – how difficult it was to get there (transportation, babysitting, mental health problems, etc., we could write the book on problems). Refusing to energize the negative, we reflect to them the fact they chose to be in group (what they are doing that's positive) and what they could have chosen instead (what they are not doing)…that they could have chosen to go out and use substances today and they made a choice to be in group instead.

The journey has been marked with absolute resistance from the substance abuse treatment providers. In fact, the journey was downright miserable at times. However, both my co-facilitator and I remained fearless and relentless in using the Nurtured Heart Approach. Our CPS and Mental Health supervisors went to the mat for us. We were truly blessed to have them. I am thoroughly convinced the miraculous results were realized by relentlessly using the Nurtured Heart Approach. We have been fearless in attending to and electrifying success.

We do not have to search for success. It is right under our noses. It took a dramatic paradigm shift away from my classical mental health/substance abuse training to actually 'see' what was there all along: the strength, the power and the goodness of the individual rather than the 'problem.' Most systems in the mental health/substance abuse fields focus on identifying and fixing problems. I was certainly trained in this manner. What a relief to go on a treasure hunt of a person's wealth of goodness! I often tell others that it is my job to "go for the jugular of a person's goodness."

A question I always get from naysayers is, "What do you do when someone in the group admits to using or has a positive drug test?" I know what the usual approach is: to get all jazzed up, call the person in for a session (even better, a network meeting with all the treatment professionals, social workers, etc.) to rake them over the coals, and more frequently than not, kick them out of the substance abuse program for breaking the rules.

❧

I had to learn first-hand the power of the Nurtured Heart Approach from a client. This particular woman was on her last legs with CPS. Angela was referred to me after being in the system for almost 18 months and was not only in danger of having her services terminated, she was in danger of having her parental rights terminated as well. She had a long history of substance abuse treatment, yet she continued to use drugs regularly and her children had been placed in long-term foster care. Because she continued using, there was little hope of having the children reunified.

Angela could have been described as a therapist's worst nightmare. Previously diagnosed with borderline personality disorder and armed with a 20-year history of crystal methamphetamine abuse, she was able to eloquently, fluently and precisely blame her parents, her children, her ex-spouse, her previous therapists and her previous substance abuse treatment providers for her numerous failures. Nonetheless, I saw an intellectually astute woman who could fully itemize and give evidence for her failure. What if, I thought, her intensity could be shifted – transformed as a powerful force in her favor?

In the first four months of treatment, it was evident this lovely woman was benefiting from being nurtured. She came to group. She was on time. If she was going to miss, she called to tell me. She was brilliant in her observations in the group discussion. Yet she continued to get positive drug tests for crystal methamphetamine.

On one occasion when she came to the CPS offices for her regular drug test, Angela was informed by the social worker that a previous test had come back 'dirty.' The ranting and raving began. "I don't know how that test could be dirty, I don't remember using, I must have multiple personality disorder, someone must have slipped something into my lemonade," and on it went. She demanded to see her therapist (me). Taking a fearless approach, I informed the social worker I would see Angela the following Monday in the regular group session. It seemed that scheduling an impromptu network meeting and/or an additional individual therapy session might have the effect of energizing negativity. I was not willing to energize the negativity associated with the dirty drug test.

On that Monday, a miracle occurred as this woman took a courageous leap of faith. When it was her turn to check in, she announced, "Good morning, my name is Angela and I got a dirty drug test because I used." My immediate response was, "Oops, bummer; broke a rule. I am sure you are going to have a consequence for using; however, I have to accuse you of being such an honest person. Right now I am sincerely appreciating your honesty. I also have to accuse you of having integrity. You could have yelled and screamed and blamed everything and everyone for this dirty test, but you are not. You are taking responsibility, you are being completely honest, and you are giving me irrefutable evidence you are a woman of integrity. Now how many hours have you been clean and sober???" She responded it had been about 72 hours. I don't know what landed in this woman's heart that day or how. I do know she had that strange look on her face that happens when a person 'gets it,' and the transformation is irrefutably imbedded and fully in motion.

(As a footnote, the group discussion took a delightful twist at this juncture. One woman ventured, "I just thought of something. Before I started using, I had 15 years of practice being clean and sober." Another spoke up, "That reminds me, too. I had 18 years of practice being clean before I tried crystal meth for the first time." Each woman in the group chimed in with her own years of successful sobriety. What a powerfully sobering concept that was for me as a co-facilitator.)

From this group session on, Angela did not test dirty again. Her growth was demonstrably exponential. Four months later, she reunited with her children; even the judge was stunned at the complete transformation he witnessed in his courtroom. He dismissed her case without the customary six months to one year of family maintenance. To this day, she remains clean and sober and is parenting her children in a loving and responsible manner. She is a miracle. She taught me over and over that recovery is not just about not using drugs and/or alcohol; it is about retrieving and recovering the authentic self.

In one group session, a client asked me, "Susan, I am curious. Why do you use the word 'accuse' when you are complimenting us?" Before I had a chance to respond, another woman in the group spoke up: "I know why. When Susan draws the picture of the brain on the board, she shows us how the neuronal pathways have been damaged or broken because of the drug use, the trauma or the drama. She uses the word 'accuse' to access and open an existing pathway, and then the compliment that follows behind the accusation heals the pathway." At that moment, I was the one in tears, truly appreciating the tremendous wisdom being expressed. I am looking forward to the day when the research proves this hypothesis to be true.

From the inception of our Seeking Safety/Nurtured Heart group, my co-facilitator and I have worked with many, many women. We have been transfixed as we have repeatedly witnessed the moment to moment to moment transformation of individuals who were once thought to be and presented as unreachable, un-teachable and treatment-resistant. But everyone with whom we have worked has given explicit evidence of the intrinsic goodness and the divinity that resides within their heart and soul. One woman has become an author (two of her books are in the publication stage), and several have returned to college pursuing degrees in chemistry, radiology, the helping professions and other intensive fields. Many live dedicated lives appreciating the simple pleasures that exist in honoring and nurturing self, family members and others.

When I left the week-long Nurtured Heart intensive training, I made a personal commitment that I would never practice 'therapy' again, that I would only practice transformation. As a result of that commitment, I am completely re-energized in my work. I no longer have any thought or desire to leave the mental health profession. Words cannot adequately express my newfound passion and excitement.

When I graduated from my master's program, our keynote speaker gave a very short yet poignant appeal: "Go out and make a difference." As illusive as that dream seemed earlier in my career, finally, and through the Nurtured Heart Approach, that dream is now my reality.

Susan Redford is a Master's level dually licensed mental health and substance abuse therapist. The Nurtured Heart Approach is the foundation for all her work. She has witnessed the transformation in individuals, couples and even her own grandchildren. Her work has come to the attention of the state leadership who are abuzz with the successful outcomes of a treatment that 'really works.' In less than a year, eight Nurtured Heart/Seeking Safety groups were under way in the area, pioneered by the vision of Susan and her co-worker Kathy Baker.

This is the first time I have heard of the Nurtured Heart Approach used in this manner; i.e., with a notoriously challenging and under-supported population. Susan's expansion of the Nurtured

Heart Approach to adult drug rehabilitation and CPS counseling support is a sparkling example of creatively expanding this approach into a healing paradigm beyond children.

Susan is masterful with her focus on refusing to energize negativity while handing out abundant Recognitions and Appreciations for her clients' integrity. This arrow of truth and love becomes almost a finger-snap method to break through and bring heart and esteem issues up to be healed. Equally miraculous are the results and low recidivism/relapse rate.

I absolutely love Susan's fearless resolve to use the approach, even as a novice, and her ability to forge ahead in the face of potential intimidation. How many professionals have all but given up, burned out or yelled back in response to the fear-based negatives and armored veneers of clients like these? Instead, Susan and her co-worker Kathy were able to see the miracles waiting to happen. They were able to take a totally different approach and bring out the true good person, which began the transformations. JLE

I have now read this story at least six times and each time I marvel at nuances that take my breath away. For example, I really agree that 'accusing' someone of greatness enters the heart on another pathway. As a society, it is clear that drama sells, and so much of the media bases its approach on how drama keeps people buying tickets and spellbound. The problem is that media's drama is mostly about pain and aggression. Susan and Kathy turn drama on its end and engage the same gears through 'accusing' these women of success and greatness — but of equal importance, at the same time they refuse to enter into the realm of negativity. This is a pivotal stance, especially given that so many of those on a substance-abusing path have a drama script in spades and revel in negativity.

In fact, refusing to enter into relationship around negativity and refusing to lend energy to these endeavors clearly give Susan and Kathy an even greater platform to rally accusations of success. By being this conscious and determined when a group member begins a rant or an excuse, they can listen in a *completely different way that opens up numerous possibilities of creating statements of success. They clearly demonstrate in this remarkable story that those statements are always there and that these women who were previously deemed impervious to treatment can be so amazingly responsive to their greatness. It's as if this greatness in them was always there just waiting to be appreciated. And once unearthed, it begins to bloom and have a life of its own.*

I am so impressed with the groundbreaking work that Susan and Kathy have ignited, and so thrilled to hear of the support they are getting within the Child Protective Services and justice systems. This is truly the fruit of their amazing efforts and the greatness of their wisdom, tenacity and purpose. HNG

Tyrone

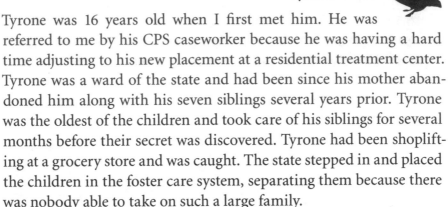

By Lisa Bravo

Tyrone was 16 years old when I first met him. He was referred to me by his CPS caseworker because he was having a hard time adjusting to his new placement at a residential treatment center. Tyrone was a ward of the state and had been since his mother abandoned him along with his seven siblings several years prior. Tyrone was the oldest of the children and took care of his siblings for several months before their secret was discovered. Tyrone had been shoplifting at a grocery store and was caught. The state stepped in and placed the children in the foster care system, separating them because there was nobody able to take on such a large family.

Needless to say, Tyrone was very traumatized by the circumstances of his life. He had disrupted several foster placements in the first few years and had become aggressive and sometimes violent. This residential treatment center was the 'end of the line' for Tyrone and he knew it. Tyrone was very obese and had a speech impediment. He was teased by the other boys in his residence and often turned to books to escape the misery of his life. He was very bright despite his lack of formal schooling and would often challenge the authority of some of the staff at the center. This behavior often landed him in detention and he was not exactly a 'favorite' among the staff.

My first encounter with Tyrone was in my office. He was talking loudly – demanding of the receptionist to know how long he would have to wait to be seen. When I went to greet him, he was pacing and agitated. He followed me to my office and went on about how his transportation was late, he was thirsty and I was running late. I actively recognized him for his ability to hold it together and pointed out his articulate communication skills. He calmed down almost immediately. I saw him two more times with similar scenarios. He would get himself wound up in the lobby and come into my office with both guns blazing. I would spend the bulk of our session deescalating him. I had been using the techniques of the Nurtured Heart Approach with him, but it seemed I always had to calm him down first.

Tyrone taught me a valuable lesson. On some level he was creating problems so that he could have a relationship – an emotional connection – with me. He knew that if he did not have 'problems,' a lot was at stake. If he was 'well,' his CPS worker would not be in contact with him every day; he would not get to leave his program to see a counselor; there would not be the opportunity to feel nurtured or valued by another human being; he would not get to have a relationship with the receptionist; and he would not have any one-on-one interaction with the people who drove him to see me every week.

I knew that I had to change our relationship from one based on problems and drama to one based on creative solutions and manifestations of inner wealth. At the third session, I told Tyrone that from now on we were only going to talk about his brilliance. I told him that if he had a problem he wanted to discuss, he would have to first decide on a solution before bringing it to our session. With consistent coaching and refusal to engage in his attempts at being negative, Tyrone learned to 'reset' himself and look at every interaction as an opportunity to learn more about the gifts others see in him. Eventually he awakened to the many gifts he had within him all along. He began to look at his early life not as a tragedy, but as a launching pad to one day helping other people. Tyrone began eating healthy foods, exercising and identifying goals for himself. In the year that I knew him, he lost more than 100 pounds and decided he wanted to become a pediatrician. The last time I spoke with Tyrone, he had enrolled in college and was a pre-med major.

This experience with Tyrone changed the way I conducted my practice and completely changed the way I do therapy. As I honed my skill at implementing the Nurtured Heart Approach, I began to see that significantly fewer children needed medication, there were shorter stays in therapy and my clients were undeniably able to generalize their greatness to other areas of their lives. Before my eyes, these parentless children began to parent and nurture themselves – to take control of their own lives, to make better choices, to think about their futures. The more they experienced successes through positive daily choices, the more they created first-hand experiences of success and the more emotionally wealthy they became.

Lisa's powerful story conveys the visionary shift that comes from connecting to strengths and greatness rather than problems or the legacy of negative history. Courageously, Lisa literally cuts a standard therapeutic cord that potentially feeds problem-driven negativity and shifts the lens in support of Tyrone's greatness. I believe it is this shift that fueled the miracle that occurred in the life of this young man. It called forth the energy of self-empowerment and personal integrity. What an amazing physician this young man has the potential to become! **JLE**

I totally agree with Jennifer! It's so clear from this story that falling into the trap of discussing the endless problems Tyrone could supply would forever block the emergence of the forward thrust awakening his greatness. When Lisa first met Tyrone, the sum total of his prior experiences had led him to believe that problems were the only way to experience human connection, and without problems there was no relationship.

Lisa's brilliant refusal to further propel this fruitless path, which I see as her taking the stand of a warrior, cleared the way for new pathways for this amazing young man in the exploration of his greatness. How perfect, fitting and proper that he will get to be in a profession to greatly help others.

I love that Tyrone gets to be the hero of this story through the greatness Lisa temporarily lends him. He's a hero because he eventually takes up his own cause of finding his own greatness. Lisa is also a hero because she brought forward Tyrone's path to greatness, one that could truly have gone undiscovered for a lifetime. This story thrills me to the core. This is why I see the teachers, parents and therapists who provide the initial push as such amazing and heroic people. **HNG**

Another In-School Success Story: There's No Penalty for Being on Time!

By Ellen Thomas

The 'first bell' has just rung this morning in the seventh grade hallway. Approximately 220 students are squeezing coats and back packs into their lockers. This first bell indicates that three minutes remain until the 'second bell' rings, which indicates that school is officially started. If you aren't in class and in your seat by 7:50 a.m., you're late.

When you're in middle school, you might be operating on a different time zone concept than anyone else. Certainly, your concept might not coincide at all with that of the adults. Many students linger before first hour. It's an interesting path: Stop at the restroom, talk to your friends, go to your locker, talk some more, stop by the attendance office to see who is late. Never mind that you, too, are late.

This morning, an adult voice bellows, "Get to class! You are going to be late! When you are late, that is a detention!" No one under the age of 15 will hear this important news bulletin. Linger, linger, linger. Talk, talk, talk. Again the announcement is made. Again, linger and talk.

I step into the middle of the hallway. (Most of the time, even I don't know what I'm going to do or say next. Today was no different.) But I loudly begin: "There is NO PENALTY for being on time! NO PENALTY TO ANYONE WHO IS ON TIME!" Then I approach students one by one. "Did you hear?! There's NO PENALTY for being on time!" Students look at me like I'm crazy, but they do that most days. (I think we have an understanding that I probably am somewhat off. That's what it takes to work in a middle school.) One student stops and asks, "What do you mean, there's no penalty?" I continue to carry on about how there is NO PENALTY and how cool that is! She puts her finger on her head and then says, "Ohhhh, I get it! NO PENALTY. That's pretty cool Mrs. Thomas!"

Maybe it is coincidence, but this morning when the second bell rings, only two students remain in the hallway!

Ellen is a 'middle school master/trickster' as she transcends the mundane and conventional to invent lightening-bolts of positive energy. Disdaining the 'negative-sweep-into-compliance' method, she literally showers out illumination. This becomes the sparkling new hook of attention that guides those lost in adolescent fog back to engaged flight. JLE

Ellen sidesteps the normal trap that a middle-school hallway between classes so achingly calls for: giving energy to negativity. It can happen in a heartbeat. I believe every one of us carries the gene of being so talented at seeing what is wrong with a picture. We can zero in on the smallest examples of what's not right and then be so adept at waxing poetically about those negatives. Just reading Ellen's description of this hallway scenario, I can feel in my bones an inherent desire to cry out for order and obedience. To do what Ellen does in this story takes a great dose of determination and consciousness: that she won't give way to giving energy for negativity. Ellen has surprising and unique ways of doing this – and they seem to unfailingly work. I like that she respects her own style and gets the job done. HNG

The Relationship – Ah, That's the Thing!

By Brenda Murphy

In an age where parental skepticism about 'new' behavioral approaches seems to be the coin of the realm, the Nurtured Heart Approach has proven to be remarkably effective when other methods fail. I love teaching the approach because I truly believe in it, PLUS I love teaching. As a professional Family Educator and Parent Coach, I am always delighted to hear my clients return to a follow-up session exclaiming, "It works! It works! I wasn't sure at first. I've tried so many things that worked at first, only to be disappointed after several weeks' trial. But you told me to hang in there, to stress the importance of the relationship instead of seeing only the behavior. And then it happened, my child's behavior has changed and I can't believe it! I'm so happy now. Our family life is so much more peaceful. Thank you!"

In 2006, I received a frantic call from the mother of a young girl. This mother described intense behavior that sometimes involved hitting. She had tried everything, including health checkups and a visit to a therapist to have the child evaluated. The mother was frustrated because the therapist recommended she read a book. She had already read a mountain of books and articles and she understood theory, but not the practical aspects of how to make things work.

My practice emphasizes the practical 'how to' aspect of parenting, which was what the mother believed had been missing for her. When I present the Nurtured Heart model, I ask parents to journey inward the first week and survey the interior landscape, noticing what beliefs they hold, especially when a behavioral issue arises. They are then asked to simply 'notice' their interaction with the child. Noticing, as I teach the model, is the first step. Once the parents get a glimpse of their own baggage, beliefs, and how these elements drive the environment, we are both on our way to implementing the model, adjusting it as needed along the way, but always with the true goal in mind: heartfelt love and gratitude for the relationship. Behavioral problems don't develop in a day and they won't be resolved in a day, either. But the relationship, ah, that's the thing!

The first week, this brave mom set her intention to stick to the plan no matter how intense or passionate the 'blow back.' She weathered the first week well and was slightly astonished at how well her child was taking to the 'new' method. I had cautioned the mom several times that the honeymoon period is short-lived, and when the novelty wears off, the child will pull out all the stops to push the parent back into the old default position where the child can once again be in charge through negativity.

This mom was prepared. She did not like the blow back, but I reminded her to stick to her plan no matter what and also to remember to breathe! The second week was awful, but mom held on tight to her vision of her ultimate goal: a child who would learn to self-manage the inner tension that drove her to explosive outbursts. This was a goal she could accomplish only by building relationship around successes and none through negativity. Again and again, I encouraged this parent to keep going and know in her heart that she would reach her goal, one minute at a time perhaps, but reach it she would.

The third week, the child began to turn the corner. She voluntarily brought her laundry down from her room without being asked. She was making a real effort to be compliant. Again, I reminded my client that consistency is the goal and the new behavior had to become the rule rather than the exception. Mom needed to be prepared for lapses, bad days, low energy, malaise, and sometimes an out-of-sorts mood for no apparent reason. These represent a spectacular opportunity for the parent to really SHINE in empathy while expecting appropriate behavior.

By the fourth week, the child had the best kind of breakthrough. She said to her mother over breakfast, "I don't know what has happened around here, but I like the new rules," and with this she smiled and left for school, happy as could be.

Nearly two years later, this gifted child is excelling in school. She self-manages her behavior well. She puts herself into the guest room where she 'thinks about' her poor choices and 'resets' herself. When she feels better, she leaves the room and announces her 'new and improved' mood. The family is thrilled.

Obviously, children will be children and no child is going to be compliant 100 percent of the time. This child manages to reach her goals the vast majority of the time and that feels right. The family now takes vacations together without fearing meltdowns or tantrums. This child is blessed to have such a strong and loving mother who was willing to walk through fire for her daughter's well being.

I have many wonderful stories, but this one makes my heart especially happy. I so appreciate intense children and exhausted parents because I've been both! As the mother of two and grandmother of four, I continue to 'practice what I preach.'

Founder and Executive Director of The Georgia Centre for Parental Coaching in Walton County, Georgia, Brenda Murphy is deeply committed to improving relationships between children and their parents not only in Georgia, but also nationwide. As the mother of two adult daughters and the grandmother of four, she regularly gets to 'practice what she preaches.' Brenda is the official patient educator/coach for a large medical center in metro Atlanta, and she works with psychotherapists in the area on a cross-referral basis.

So many parents are tested to the 'Nth' degree, especially while they are bringing their old ways of parenting to a screeching halt and substituting a brand new approach. Even though most children love the feeling of being congratulated in these more powerful ways, they are still essentially addicted to believing that they get a juicier version of relationship through adversity. The child had to pull out all the stops before she was convinced in a core way that there's no longer any energetic hold through her adversity. She figured out how to make better choices and live her life through successfulness. As this deepens, positivity becomes her new default setting.

Brenda Murphy's mantra of "relationship, relationship, relationship" is her brilliant reminder to herself and those she helps to put that single factor above all else in the moment to moment decisions of how to respond. Brenda's utter clarity not to taint that relationship by giving any energy to negativity guides her work and, in this story, leads this mom and daughter to a new realm of connectedness. Brenda lends this family great support when the going gets rough. HNG

Brenda's coaching strategies honor and fortify the most essential dynamic in the Nurtured Heart Approach — the relationship, and aspects of trust and support that flow from that place. This refusal to revert back to old patterns of negativity is really the power juice here, with compassion as a benevolent companion. Brenda offers wise preparation to this parent: to expect the inevitable testing as well as the possibility of relapse. This mother's unflappable intention literally calls forth the success steps. She is prepared with fortitude and the means for consistency. Both become the mixture and mortar of connection and change for her child. JLE

A New Michael

By Debi Sementelli

The call was typical: A frantic mom concerned about her son's behavior in school. They'd been getting the dreaded 'notes from the teacher' for awhile now. The school had strongly suggested that their first-grade son needed play therapy. He was not getting along well with others, including his teachers. Instead, the parents contacted me. (In addition to being a parent coach and trainer, I'd been through a similar situation and had successfully utilized the Nurtured Heart Approach with my youngest child. Working with elementary kids for 12 years and teaching parenting classes and workshops for 14, I've seen many boys struggle to fit in the classroom.)

After spending a day doing a school observation of their son Michael, I could understand both sides. I could see how his behaviors agitated his peers and caused him to be perceived as disrespectful to his teachers. I could also see a bright boy who was doing the best he could with what he had.

Every teacher I spoke with made note of how he always argued with them. They all felt challenged by that. Even after being corrected, he continued to use the same inappropriate behavior. His physical boundaries were lacking. He seemed to want to always be touching someone or get as physically close as he could. The overall sense I got from his teachers was a lack of respect. His behavior on the playground tended to be aggressive. He wanted to have things his way or no way. He wanted to win all the time. He went so far as to pull a girl's hair to keep her from scoring a soccer goal. Even in a situation where he didn't really know the actual details of the game being played, he would call kids "out" and argue about the rules.

As I observed him, he appeared oblivious to the fact that the teacher was talking as he continually chatted with the student next to him. He regularly spoke out of turn without raising his hand and was somewhat directive with the teacher when he wanted her to do something. When a parent of another student poked her head into the classroom, he immediately informed this parent that her son was not successful at a math game they'd done on the computer earlier, completely unaware of how inappropriate he was being.

At the same time, I could see the boy that his parents described: smart, enthusiastic, outgoing, articulate, quick witted, funny and sensitive to others who might be hurting. As I stated to his parents, "He's like a little elf; bright, funny and full of life." What was missing were boundaries and skills to help him be all those good things without being disrespectful to others. As I believe with most kids, it's not a matter of being bad or good. It's a matter of being shown what is and isn't appropriate, being taught the skills needed to apply that information and being given the opportunity to practice and fine-tune that application.

When I shared my observations with Michael's parents, I could feel their heavy hearts. They wanted to help him be all he could be and still have healthy and appropriate boundaries with others. I could not have asked for more dedicated and committed parents. They were ready and willing to put my suggestions into action.

I introduced them to the Nurtured Heart Approach. They checked out the website and began reading the book. His teacher was enthusiastic about "trying anything" that might help. When we met, I could sense the relief in her voice when she realized how little time it would take from her already busy school day. Before long, we were off and running.

We made a Nurtured Heart-based School Points chart for Michael. It included rules such as: No rolling on floor or falling down; No talking unless you raise your hand; No arguing with teachers or other kids; and Keep your hands and feet to yourself. He would receive points (or credits) for following the rules, along with 'gimmies' for behaviors he was already successful at: participating in class, lining up nicely, turning in homework and following directions. Bonus points were given for good behavior on the playground and in other settings.

In addition to helping them implement the components of the Nurtured Heart Approach, I also suggested a Special Skills Chart, a recommendation I make to all the parents of young children. Here is what I tell them. Trace your child's body on a large sheet of craft paper and have him color himself in and put his name at the top along with the words 'Special Skills.' Tell him you're going to keep track of all the skills he has, new and old. Start by asking them what they do well. Jump high? Run fast? Whatever they say, write it down. Then every night before they go to bed, ask them to tell you something else they do well or have learned to do that they couldn't do before. Take turns playing? Help with dinner? Whatever they say gets written on the chart. As the days go on, you can help them identify the 'new' skills they are learning: stay in their seat at school, raise their hand to speak, etc. Reading all of the skills that are written on the chart every night creates a nightly 'boost' of healthy self-esteem.

The goal is to not only help them to see themselves as capable and significant, but their parents as well. Ending the day focusing on the good things that your child is doing gives you the motivation to keep putting forth the positive energy needed to give her the training and skills she so desperately needs. As Howard Glasser points out, "If you water the weeds, the weeds will grow. If you water the flowers, the flowers will grow."

With the help of affirmations throughout the day from his teacher, within a few weeks Michael's behavior changed for the better. All of his teachers commented on the new ways that he was responding. His main teacher said he was like a new Michael! With the aid of a positively focused system, the energy of two very diligent parents and the help of a teacher who was open to re-directing her energy in a new way, he was exactly who he was supposed to be.

Thank you, Debi, for your wonderful story of transformation. This is a story of unhooking from the non-productive, insidious negatives. It is a new vision of seeing and healing Michael by nurturing his strengths and gifts, not the weak spots! Michael, his parents and the school were stuck in an environment of heavy negatives, searching for a way out.

Bless these parents for showing the courage to seek change for Michael and themselves! Michael, the exuberant Elf Boy, benefited greatly from the unified approach between parents and school (as do all children). It is testimony to the necessary blend of linking all a child's life supports to the task of unhooking her from negative energy and focusing all her energy and attention to affirm and nourish positive connections.

The positive power of a credit system and special skills chart represented the healing crucible here, no doubt. This provided a new course for all, to everyone's benefit. JLE

I love that Debi teaches parents not to 'water the weeds.' And one great way to make huge headway in this direction is to be truly devoted to 'watering the flowers.' Debi has devised many creative methods and products that introduce and secure this nurturing process as a way of life rather than a way of merely managing behavior. She's truly brilliant in helping parents, teachers and children see and cherish their greatness. HNG

Four Snapshots of Success

By Michele Greenish

These are windows of transformation from parents in my workshops. We meet for six weeks, four hours weekly, in small groups of 10-12 people. Nearly all have challenging children, and all are entering a new realm in parenting – learning the Nurtured Heart Approach. Once they get over their initial skepticism, parents are shocked at their success. Several came forth to share the windows of success described below. In these 'snapshots of success,' the parents demonstrate their heartfelt determination to turn things around and literally trick their children into success, each in his or her own manner.

Snapshot #1 – Active Recognition: The Morning After

The first vignette comes from Laura and her son Alex. On her first day of implementing the Nurtured Heart Approach techniques at home, this mom's intervention was superb. In the following days, she would discover the power of giving nutritious attention, recognition and applause to her son in order to get the success going. In addition, she intuitively found a way to make her requests bullet-proof, a strategy we would learn but not until a later session.

At her first session in our group, Laura told us about Alex. "Getting my 8-year-old up and ready for school in the morning is a circus. He is in a bad mood, has temper tantrums, and jumps up and down on furniture. By the time he leaves for school, I am totally frustrated and exhausted before the day has even begun. I am at my wit's end with this child."

During the very next breakfast episode after Laura's first session in our group, defiant Alex starts his usual antics. Laura tells us: "I am about to loose it with him when this brilliant idea flashes through my mind from our discussion and exercises with Video Moments and Freeze Framing. I remember to shift from 'you' to 'I' statements when I start a sentence. Instead of blurting out my usual 'You stop that jumping right now,' I hear myself saying very matter-of-factly, 'Alex, I need you to stop jumping on the couch and I need you to come and sit at the table now.' Alex is so stunned to hear me speak this way to him; he would probably have stayed up in mid-air if gravity would not have brought him back down. He looks at me intently and says 'Mom, how are you talking to me!?' Still stunned by the change he sees, he proceeds to sit down and eat his breakfast without any fuss!"

Like Alex, I was stunned by what had happened and absolutely shocked by the power for change this simple tool exacted so quickly. Where this mother had seen Alex as an impossible kid to raise and had felt frustrated and helpless at the task, everything changed. She told me: "All of a sudden I could envision myself as an agent of change with a real chance to pull Alex and us, his parents, into new patterns of success. I could feel a renewed, heartfelt commitment toward my child to do what it takes to pull him in the direction of that success. That was a very empowering realization."

        ♾

I love that Michele shares with us the delight she experienced over the power and immediacy of such simple Nurtured Heart tools! In the midst of this mother's despair, Michele offers the means, and the mother leaps into being an agent of change with her son. Alex feels his mother's powerful stance and immediately responds with dramatic compliance. How wonderful! JLE

There's more than one way to move a mountain. This mother has her transformative moment of resolve when she clearly decides not to enter into giving relationship and energy to negativity in the old way. The choice point may have called for a consequence or in this case a quantum leap to a request designed to create success. What really matters at the very heart of this energetic juncture is that this child perceived that his mother was no longer available in the old ways and that her shift was inviting, instantly understandable and non-negotiable.

I believe parents cannot take a stand such as the one taken here without first fully understanding some of the basic notions of this approach as well as what's truly wrong with normal parenting and what's really at stake. So bravo to Michelle for getting these concepts communicated, and bravo to this mom for

Snapshot # 2 – Active Recognition: "You Are Naïve…."

I had just started to introduce a group of parents to the Nurtured Heart Approach's superb blend of structure and consistent positive recognition for success when the father of 5-year-old David loudly interrupted me in mid-sentence. Rolling his eyes, he quipped: "Of course we reward him when he does something good, but he never does anything good; we have to punish him all the time. This kid has pushed the envelope beyond the acceptable. You are naïve to believe that your method will work with a child like ours!" His wife was silent, but the frustration of dad being at his rope's end with his son was coming out in an intense way. At first, I think he might stomp out of the class, but he stays and even participates in the Video Moments exercises. He leaves the session still doubtful about the capacity for change that might be possible by using Active Recognitions with his son at home.

Mom and Dad returned the next week with broad smiles on their faces and ecstatic to report. For the first time in five years, their son listened to them and obeyed when asked to do something. David had noticed the change in his parents, became much more affectionate with them and even said: "Dad, I like it when you talk to me like that." The power of Active Recognitions to re-establish a measure of trust in the family motivated the parents to work extremely well with the Nurtured Heart Approach for the entire the workshop. They became such an asset to the class. Dad was still very vocal, but in a very helpful way.

———————————— ⟨♡⟩ ————————————

I absolutely love Michele's classic short on how magic happens, despite parental reluctance and even a very rigid way of seeing the child through a negative lens. Although this father presents like one who may have been an intense child himself, he, too, is shifted by the focus on and use of a positive lens in the course of Michele's class. JLE

There's so much magic in the initial shift to enacting recognitions that often neither the parent nor child fully knows what hit them – other than how good it feels and the allure of wanting to continue. Don't ever discount this magic and it's power to bring an adult to WANT to stay away from connecting through negativity. Once you experience the 'promised land,' you really do want to build a home there! HNG

———————————————— 🫂 ————————————————

Snapshot # 3 – Proactive/Creative Recognitions: Tricking Dan into Following Rules

Even though Dan gets lots of negatives for it, he keeps jumping up and down on the living room sofa. Just as he's starting his next jumping frenzy, Mom catches him and holds him down by the arm. Dan is caught off guard. Before he has any chance to recuperate from the surprise effect of her move and start yelling at her, she quickly creates a Proactive Recognition move of her own brand: "I can see that you are tempted to keep jumping up and down on the couch right now. I appreciate that you follow directions and I see how well you can control your frustration right now. You are not yelling, you are not throwing yourself on the floor." (Mom is still holding him firmly by the hand, mind you.) "I appreciate that, good job." Dan tries to argue, albeit a bit hesitantly, with "I was on the couch…."

Mom is determined to trick Dan into success. She has learned that tying the control to specific rules that have not yet been broken (he hasn't yet thrown himself on the floor cursing and yelling, for example) strengthens Dan's sense of being on track: "Well, I do see these two little feet on the floor now, don't you?" Dan loves a good sense of humor. They both laugh 'heartfully.'

———————————————— 🫂 ————————————————

Another delightful vignette from Michele in which she shares the power of creating positives by not getting hooked by the negatives. What a superbly creative mother to see the opening and enact this strategy in the moment! Dan seemed to love being tricked into success by his mother and literally unhooked from his negative jumping dance. This story honors a mother who is testimony to managing ruthless intent and fortitude through firmness – all with a playful tone irresistible to her son! JLE

This mom totally gets the TRUTH of the NOW, and knows what to do with it. She has clearly decided to build the momentum by brilliantly 'stealing' a moment of success – giving herself the great vantage point of being able to communicate how grateful she is for Dan's great choice. She provides the proof.

I can't help but believe that Michele inspires this brilliance and cutting edge 'larceny.' Taking a warrior-like stance truly contributes in a powerful way to transforming the moment of truth where the child sees that all the aliveness is now for positivity and no longer for negativity. That's the momentous occasion we are fighting for! HNG

Snapshot # 4 – Creative Recognition and the Power of the Heart

The saying goes that we teach what we need to learn or relearn. I am watching an animated group of parents entering into the room for their fourth session. I wonder which of their stories will help form the lesson for this session. They are chatting and freely exchanging notes, comments and good moods with each other. I can't help thinking what a difference three weeks of working with the program has made for them. It's such a contrast with the first session when they had walked into the class feeling low, depressed and angry, carrying inside of them versions of the same sense of helplessness, the same pain of feeling that they were utterly losing the emotional bond to their children.

Margot had baked an apricot pie for the group. I notice that she's carrying Howard's Nurtured Heart book against her – as if holding it for dear life, like they all do. I don't know it yet, but later her story will be a powerful reminder of the truth I cherish and teach about transformation and change: The skillful use of the tools, no matter their brilliance, is only part of the magic of success. Real, lasting change comes when what we are doing gets in line with the power of the heart. Feelings from the heart give us respect for the integrity of our children. As she shared this profound lesson with us, it became the all-important one for Margot and her son.

We started the session sharing how the week went practicing Creative Recognitions at home, making requests bullet-proof and setting tasks where it is virtually impossible, even for an obnoxious and uncooperative child, to fail. They are excited to share how masterfully they had created success when very little good could otherwise be found through the day.

Margot shared her success story, adding a zest of 'when everything else fails' from the book and a good dose of benevolence toward her son. It happens that Tim never closes the door of the refrigerator properly. So she decides to buy some cans of Coca-Cola for him. (Sweet drinks were not normally allowed at her house but she totally trusts that the book will offer a new solution later to elicit compliance without the coke factor.) Next time Tim is in the kitchen, Mom says, "Go get yourself a Coke…" Tim gleefully complies and is in the act of closing the door when Mom delivers a simple and direct request: "I need you to push the door all the way closed" – which is a done deal, as Tim is in a very cooperative mood at this point.

Mom follows with applause. "I appreciate when you follow my direction and close the door completely so well." She continued to make other extremely doable requests of Tim, all followed by heartfelt applause and all yielding the same positive outcome.

As we listen to her, it becomes more and more clear to all that Margot has deliberately found a powerful way to connect the tone of her voice, the look in her eyes and the expression in her face to her heart. She is now able to communicate the sincerity of her benevolent intention and goodwill to her son and give him concrete evidence of the esteem in which he is held. That is Margot's lesson of the heart to all of us. Success!

As a clinician, a therapist and a mother of three who raised a family in different cultures over three continents, Michele Greenish is adamant about the Nurtured Heart Approach. "I have found no other approach that could, would or did equal its brilliant efficacy to parent challenging children like our first born." She is now a Certified Nurtured Heart Specialist offering workshops in Europe where her family presently resides.

Margot reflects to us the deeper magic and power that comes from inner alignment between heart-full intent and words. By applying the Nurtured Heart Approach, this mother's heart is holding the child in deepest esteem, regard and gratitude. Thank you, Michele, for helping this mother in a little seen but powerful transformation of loosening her energy within. JLE

I was on a phone consultation just prior to reading Margot's story and trying to explain the need for a higher trajectory of positives and the way to do it. It's not always easy to explain, especially over the phone, how to bring the feeling of gratefulness and appreciation into the heart and have it not merely be a cognitive exercise. I personally like connecting the rhythm of my breath with the rhythm of my heart and then I know I'm at least close (Google Heart-Rhythm Meditation). Engaging the gear of the heart makes our compliments infinitely more powerful. I'm convinced the child perceives these at an entirely different level. The heart is both a transmitter of signals and a receiver. And so, to the extent that the trajectory is altered to making the positive a more powerful experience, the absence of energy and relationship to negativity is commensurately more powerful as well. HNG

Another In-School Success Story: Need a Ride?

By Ellen Thomas

Terrence struggles everyday to get to class. The seventh-grader likes to stop by my classroom to see how I'm doing. He really doesn't want to go to class. "Nooo, I don't want to go! Pleeeez don't make me go!" There's plenty of good-natured drama. But I can't let him avoid it. He must want a little pleasant interaction, and what I needed to do was find a way to give him that interaction but still get him to class.

This day, as usual, he comes to my door. "How ya doin' Mrs. Thomas? You doin' good?" I am ready. "Hey Terrence, I am great! You need a ride to class? C'mon, I'll drive!" He looks at me, confused. I tell him to hop in because we are going to carpool to class. He is trying to resist, but I hold up my coffee mug and tell him I just had the oil changed in the 'car.'

The 'drive' to first hour isn't long – his class is only a few doors down from my room. During our 'ride' I'm telling him how great I think it is that he chooses to carpool, how ecologically responsible it is. He goes along with my ploy beautifully. I also tell him that it's awesome that he has his materials and "brought them along on the ride." I continue to douse my passenger with words about how pre-pared he is and how willing he is to get to first hour. As we arrive at his classroom, I make a screeching sound as if I'm putting on the brakes. "Well, this is your stop," I say. "Beep! Beep!" is his reply. We both get what we want. I want him to be in class, and on time. He wants someone to pay attention to him. "Hey, Mrs. Thomas," Terrence asks. "What's up with the big dent in your passenger side door?" I smile and say, "Hey man, I know it's dented, I know it's old, but it gets me where I want to go!" "Well, beep, beep Mrs. Thomas. Can I have a ride tomorrow?"

From that day on, we 'carpooled' most days. Some days Terrence offered to 'drive.' Once when he was wearing a new sweatshirt and sneakers, I commented that he had gotten his 'car' detailed. He said, "Yeah, Mrs. Thomas, new upholstery, even new tires. What do you think?" My reply: "Terrence, your car looks just fabulous! You obviously take the time to drive a nice ride. You're following the rules of the road, you are under the speed limit of the seventh-grade hallway, AND you have all your supplies with you in the passenger seat. You've got such a good driving record!"

Ellen's delightful story gives new meaning to transporting someone by way of the Nurtured Heart Approach! Refusing to be hooked by the obvious negatives, she creatively uses her skill to move Terrence to where he needs to go, showering him with Recognitions and Acknowledgements for any positives she can think of as they 'drive' to the desired destination. I wish we had all had such creative middle-school mentors as Ellen! Bravo to the queen of Creative Recognitions! JLE

A second bravo to Ellen! Reading the beginning of the story, it is so clear that she could have succumbed to fear and simply maintained the status quo, as many of us would have. She avoided worry, misery and doubt (both hers and Terrence's) – typically the primary emotions that foster energy and relationship in response to negativity. Instead, she fearlessly and beautifully devised a way to lead Terrence down the new road of positivity and success. To me she was driving a Rolls Royce! HNG

Allie's Story

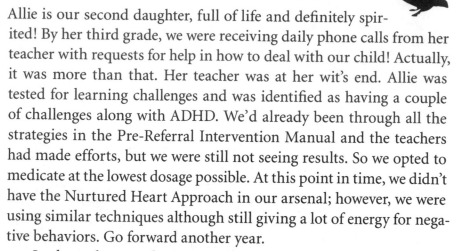

By Jan Hunter

Allie is our second daughter, full of life and definitely spirited! By her third grade, we were receiving daily phone calls from her teacher with requests for help in how to deal with our child! Actually, it was more than that. Her teacher was at her wit's end. Allie was tested for learning challenges and was identified as having a couple of challenges along with ADHD. We'd already been through all the strategies in the Pre-Referral Intervention Manual and the teachers had made efforts, but we were still not seeing results. So we opted to medicate at the lowest dosage possible. At this point in time, we didn't have the Nurtured Heart Approach in our arsenal; however, we were using similar techniques although still giving a lot of energy for negative behaviors. Go forward another year.

In the early part of 1998, I read the first couple of chapters in the book *Transforming the Difficult Child* and I was hooked! We couldn't wait to get started and began implementing the Recognitions. What a difference!

It didn't take very long before we were hearing the following: "Mom, how come you're not yelling at me when I do something bad?" Or "Mom, aren't you going to get mad at me anymore?" My reply was: "Your dad and I would rather not yell at you anymore when you break a rule. We'd rather share the good stuff we see you doing when you're doing it! How would you feel about that?" It took her by surprise for sure, and of course she had to test the new boundaries, at which she was proficient.

Allie and her brother Mike, the two youngest in our family of seven children, were both extremely challenging and competitive for our attention. But not much more than a couple of weeks after initiating the Recognitions, we had the opportunity to celebrate a whole week of no fighting between Allie and Mike as they readied for school. They hadn't even realized we had noticed! But their eyes were gleaming and their hearts were pretty puffed as we cleared the table to have some root beer floats as part of a celebratory after-school treat!

Another daily problem with Allie was her meltdowns during homework sessions. Our greatest challenge at home was to get through the pile of assignments each afternoon and evening. Allie was experiencing medication re-bound during homework time. We had to get pretty inventive to make sure we could make it through her piles of work, some that she simply did not finish at school. On certain days, her frustrations just provoked a whopper of a meltdown.

Rather than let her get to that point, I suggested she take a breather in her room for a few minutes and relax before we started the next assignment. That didn't go over very well, especially since she was really hoping for the excitement that a meltdown garnered. She left the table, yelling, screaming and crying! I decided to turn this into an opportunity for Recognitions, so I followed her a moment later and knocked on her door. "I just wanted to let you know that you did something very amazing just now. You accepted my suggestion to take a break. You walked down the hallway, no stomping and no hitting the walls. You didn't even slam the door when you got to your room. WOW! You were really upset and look at all the wonderful ways you chose to be powerful!" I remember her tears subsiding and a smile appearing on her face. What a difference from earlier meltdowns! Within a few minutes, she was ready to come out and tackle the rest of her homework for that day. Yes, there were still occasional meltdowns, but she recovered faster and her self-initiated time-outs became shorter. She was well on her way to transformation.

Fast forward to 2007: Allie graduated from high school in 2004 with a regular diploma. She has a family of her own and also provides daycare for a friend's three children. She draws upon the skills she learned as she recognizes many traits very familiar to her. She is helping her friend learn and apply the Nurtured Heart Approach techniques. What a joy to know that the approach has transcended another generation and the message continues to spread.

—————————————— ♡ ——————————————

What a joy it is to read Jan's flashback to Allie's childhood! Jan shows us how she came to recognize the negative nutrition and energy that were happening for misbehavior and how to instead spotlight Allie's strengths. This is such a powerful moment in a parent's vision!

I love Jan's description of how the hearts of Allie and her brother Mike were "pretty puffed" as they experienced the reward of unhooking themselves from unproductive behaviors.

How satisfying that Allie, now a new mother of her own, is living the Nurtured Heart legacy learned from Jan through those difficult years. Allie's child is really lucky to have a mother who's been there and a grandmother like Jan, who helped forge a new generational legacy of family healing! *JLE*

The part of this story that really struck me were Jan's words to Allie immediately after suggesting that her daughter take a break. Jan refused to give an ounce of energy to the negativity that rivets most adults; rather, she deeply appreciated out loud to Allie all the things she could have done when upset BUT WASN'T in this moment. Telling the truth of this moment is a tremendously powerful tool to help us avoid the many subtle and blatant traps of giving relationship to negativity. The corner is turned when the child comes to see that she no longer has to go to the trouble of acting-out to have relationship and that it is readily available for all the good things. By Jan celebrating all the good and great things Allie was doing, Allie can now have the wonderful internal version of that for the rest of her life as well as the ability to bring this gift to others. **HNG**

Tommy's Happy Dance

By Lisa Bravo

Tommy, only 4½ years old, had been seen by a prominent developmental pediatrician and psychiatrist due to "out of control behaviors" at both preschool and at home. He was diagnosed with autism, oppositional defiant disorder, and ADHD. His parents were stricken with dread and fear about their little boy's fate. They were told he would need to be on medication to control his behaviors. His parents were devastated and did not want to medicate their son. They were very fearful of the potential side effects and were desperate to find another way. The parents contacted me.

Arriving at their home for our first meeting, I was met at the door by a sweet, happy, and VERY INTENSE little boy. He busily scurried around the room to show me his favorite toys and treasures. I noticed that the more enthusiastic I became, the more engaged he became. His mother Tanya seemed so proud of her son but admitted his 'loudness' scared her. Every time I talked to his mother, Tommy would grow louder and more physical. At one point, he started jumping on the couch, purposely breaking an established rule. In a tired and resigned way, his mother said, "This happens all the time."

When I had about as much as I could take, I began plugging in the Nurtured Heart Approach while Tanya observed. As he jumped on the couch, we intentionally turned away; he immediately got off, our cue to turn back toward him and enthusiastically energize him for NOW sitting properly, for NOW caring for the couch, and for NOW being safe. We repeated this process several times. Eventually, when Tommy realized that the game was no longer about jumping – it was NOW about sitting properly – he sat contentedly and drank in his own greatness. The mother was astounded.

We then tackled the room he "always" refused to clean. His father had joined us by then and began to lament about what a chore it was to get him to clean his room. I started by energizing every tiny thing Tommy was doing well and giving no attention to any negatives. He began to clean his room piece by piece. With each success, the parents became more enthusiastic and began to energize success after success.

Soon the entire mood of the room had changed! And then a miracle happened.

As Tommy put the last truck away, I instructed the parents to do "the happy dance." The boy naturally joined the fun and, without warning, laid in the middle of our dancing circle and began to sing happy birthday to himself at the top of his lungs. His parents looked at each other, their eyes filled with tears, and said, "Okay, we get it, we get it!"

These parents were raising a very intense and physically active boy. They needed to match his level of enthusiasm, but only when he was exhibiting positive behaviors. It made all the difference. Eventually the acting-out behaviors they were so keenly aware of began to subside. The approach worked to help these parents get 'tuned in' to the language and nuances of their intense boy. By consistently implementing the approach in their home, they helped their son get 'turned on' in all the right ways.

Lisa brings us a classic image of the dread and darkness facing parents with a heavy diagnosis/prognosis like Tommy's, or those who are simply unprepared for the energy and intensity of such a powerhouse. So many parents would just give up or defer to medication as inevitable, mostly because they don't have the gift of a healer like Lisa or the personal resolve to seek a new window — ways to unhook the negative energy and engage the gears of success-building.

What an awesome moment that must have been for all when Lisa led the 'posse' into pulling energy and attention away from Tommy's negative behavior of jumping on the furniture, with dramatic and quite immediate results!

Applause to all: Tommy for feeling the success so immediately, his parents for not giving in to medication as the sole intervention, and, of course, to Lisa for bringing the good news! The happy birthday song and dance proved that even little Tommy knew a huge celebration was in order! JLE

Jennifer says it all – it truly was a "Happy Birthday" for this youngster and the parents. It was his rebirth to a new way of life. I believe all any of us ever wants is recognition of our greatness, and as parents all we ever want is to celebrate our children's greatness. It is so easy to get lost in other worlds and other words and it is so gratifying to find our way back home. HNG

There You Are, Jacob

By Dawn Duncan-Lewis

I can think of many ways the Nurtured Heart Approach assists children developmentally, but one very important way is when a child has a parent who has mental illness or substance abuse, or both. When a parent is unable for some reason to reflect goodness or greatness back to a child or to let the child know how important he is to the parent, serious malnutrition of the heart and soul will occur. This malnutrition can look like 'bad' behaviors, depression, or even mental illness. Jacob is an example of a child starved for reflection and affection.

Jacob, age 10, was one of the first students I noticed when I came to our school for children with special needs in 2003. I first saw him lying on the floor outside his classroom, in a space I would soon learn was called "The Alcove." (If a student was in the alcove, it meant he had misbehaved in class.) Jacob was lying on his stomach and looking at his outstretched palm, talking as though to something or someone in his palm. He ignored me as I walked by.

Later that day, I noticed a commotion coming from several of the school staff as they hurried toward the outside doors. One of the Instructional Assistants said to me, "Jacob's outside again." I followed the gaggle of grown-ups outside to find them spreading out, looking for Jacob. I had a hunch. This show of so many adults looking for him represented an immense amount of energy allocated to Jacob's negative behavior patterns. I asked the adults to please go inside and let me find Jacob. They looked confused and a little worried at this request, but they went inside. The principal stayed near the door in case I might need help.

I began to talk to Jacob through the bushes that lined the side of the building. I asked him if he would come see me in my office and said that I had food and juice. Soon, out came Jacob, smiling. He followed me into the building without incident or fuss.

Jacob and I had the first of many talks we would eventually have over the next two years. Jacob continued his bazaar behaviors when he was in his classroom, in the alcove, or running around the building. Sometimes I could hear him yelling a war cry as staff were bringing a seemingly "out of control" Jacob to the "Quiet Room" (a room with a thick door where an upset youth could calm himself or herself). But when he was in my office, in the face of Recognitions and Acknowledgements, he behaved more like a 'normal' child, and sometimes, quite like an adult.

I began by using Kodak Moments out loud, carefully at first. "Jacob, you look happy today" or "Where'd you get that cool shirt?" Before too long, I was able to point out strengths and celebrate his skills without causing him undo stress. Eventually, he began to tell me about his home life. Jacob was a very loyal child and would never speak negatively about his parents. So it was difficult for him to tell of his pain and the events that were happening at home.

As I used the Nurtured Heart 'noticing' skills, however, he gained the ability to discuss his home life and his feelings and to feel okay about doing that. His mom had serious mental illness and was using drugs again. There were unsafe situations at home that we had to deal with together to create safety for him. As we interacted over time, I was able to highlight some amazing aspects of the human being sitting before me.

I noticed out loud his loyalty and his desire to 'take care' of his family. Jacob told me of his positive wishes for his parents, and I told him that he would not be able to wish them such good things if those good things were not already in him. I reflected back his courage and ability to take care of himself as he told me of the night he spent on the steps of a local elementary school, attempting to find safety for himself while hoping that the adults would take care of the safety issues he and his older brother faced at home.

I continued to reflect to Jacob who I saw in him: a boy who could make up jokes, write songs, dance like Elvis, and had the courage to want to try out for basketball. As we worked together, I soon began to realize that it was also really important to show Jacob the strengths he possessed to overcome the difficulties he had weathered so far. I began to welcome the day-to-day challenges that came up for him. I saw them as opportunities to teach Jacob about himself and to teach him how to use his words to get his needs met. Whatever strengths and skills he could realize and develop at school would become important attributes he would be able to use throughout his life, whatever life brought him.

One day I asked Jacob about when he acts 'crazy,' like when he talks to himself or imaginary creatures or runs around the building. He said, "I talk to imaginary people because it helps me not think about everything else." That made total sense to me. And at that moment, I realized it was as though I was looking through a crack in a window and peeking in at the real Jacob. I felt like saying, "There you are, Jacob!" At that moment, a tear came out of my eye unannounced. It was as if I had just witnessed someone being born. Jacob looked a little surprised and said, "Don't cry!" We then laughed together at the knowledge that we were "sharing a moment."

I was faced with a dilemma. How could I introduce Jacob's teaching staff to the Jacob I was experiencing in my office? When I tried to reflect a different Jacob to them during our staff discussions, they didn't believe it. And it had become urgently important to present this different Jacob to his world because, at that moment, his mom was trying to have him committed to a mental health facility and Social Services was trying to have Jacob and his older brother removed to foster care. Jacob's future depended on him being 'seen' as who he really was rather being seen as the 'crazy kid' that he sometimes exhibited.

I asked Jacob's teachers to come to my office for meetings with Jacob. As we talked, Jacob and I highlighted out loud for the teachers his strengths and practiced his ability to use his words. Before long, his teachers began to celebrate with us the changes that were taking place in Jacob. As Jacob showed us that he was okay with being his 'other' self in the classroom, his teachers began to notice his positive behaviors out loud: "Jacob, I see you sitting calmly at your desk, waiting for your next assignment" or "Jacob, you remained calm when Josh was upset. I'll bet that was helpful to Josh as he was calming down." Soon, Jacob was being recognized as a role model by the teachers and students alike, a role he didn't seem to mind at all. The other students sought him out, clearly feeling that he was a 'safe place' as a friend.

As Jacob began to generalize the 'other Jacob' to his classroom, it turned out not be a second too soon. The request for inpatient services was dropped by the mental health organization that governs those decisions. Jacob and his brother were indeed placed in foster care, but Jacob continued to develop himself and his real voice. He had become an expert at this. Toward the end of that school year, Jacob led a meeting of the grown-ups on his team from both the school and Social Services to create a new life for him that could really meet his needs. During the meeting, those attending recognized him out loud for how "clear, calm, and assertive" he had been as he led the meeting.

Jacob was soon mainstreamed back to his neighborhood school. He came back to see us several times, and to this day, Jacob is a reminder to me and the staff of the unseen 'good stuff' that can be lying not too far beneath the surface of the behaviors we see in difficult children. He reminds us of the enormous courage possessed by children who manage to survive very difficult situations and of the importance of believing in and calling forth those capacities – perhaps even before they are readily visible to all.

Dawn Duncan-Lewis is a Child Mental Health Specialist, a Certified Nurtured Heart Specialist and a marriage and family therapist who has been in private practice since 1999 and working for Catholic Community Services since 2003.

Dawn offers us an inspiring story of an all too common occurrence – the painful path for children of mentally ill and drug abusing parents. Jacob is literally on the brink of emotional, social and life disaster – and as Dawn says, "starving for reflection" of healthy behaviors and qualities. He looks, for all practical purposes, like a child with mental illness who has lost touch with reality and its appropriate behavioral equivalents. More surreptitiously, he shows us a confused survivor who has received more attention for the crazy behaviors than for his inner resource and resilience.

Courageously and intuitively, Dawn is the leader in her well-meaning and dedicated school setting, recognizing the major doses of attention staff members are inadvertently giving Jacob for running outside. In that moment, the wheel turns in Jacob's favor. During the first crossroads step – Jacob's compliance with her request to come to her office – Dawn is initiating what will ultimately become Jacob's transformation to functional reality.

She wisely offers what he needs without rewarding or energizing any negative dynamics of his misbehavior.

This is a miracle story, really. It is a roadmap of how Dawn literally called to and cultivated this nearly broken spirit, leading him into the new, stronger patterns of presence necessary to keep him out of a mental ward and possibly a lifetime of being seen and treated as mentally ill.

The child therapist in me shed a tear with Dawn as she relays the moment she truly saw the "real Jacob" through the protective shell built from the chaos of his past. How many therapists have missed or simply never acted upon the possibility for such a rebirthing in such a pivotal moment? Thank you, Dawn, for forging new healing paths for other healers and educators. And bravo to Jacob for realizing you can show the real you and be greater and bigger in the world! JLE

This is an absolutely thrilling story. Jacob is the new poster boy for all children's underlying greatness, just waiting to be recognized and nurtured. I contend that this greatness is not only there for the wildest, saddest and most despairing children like Jacob, but for every child.

Jacob had grown so accustomed to living on the crumbs of experiencing relationship, and then only through adversity. He desperately needed to be reminded of who he really was – a fine young person with many and varied qualities of greatness. It's one thing to tell someone they are great, but quite another to skillfully lead that person to seeing the truth of its existence. Congratulations, Dawn, on being that immensely skillful person. Equally impressive is how Dawn was able to demonstrate Jacob's new outlook of success to all the others caught in the old quagmire of negativity. By experiencing that others truly believed in him, Jacob came to believe in himself. This is the part that will remain forever, long after he graduates into the life of his own construction. HNG

Story from a Musical Mother

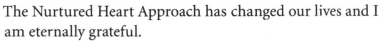

Author Anonymous

The Nurtured Heart Approach has changed our lives and I am eternally grateful.

I am the mother of an active, bright 6-year-old boy whom we adopted from birth. He is a great kid, but somewhere along the way, we lost control over him; the harder we tried to recapture it, the more discordant our relationship with him became. I read many books that I thought might help and tried many facets of this-method-or-that to figure out what we were doing wrong. Some of it was helpful, but the core problems still permeated our lives.

We were exhausted from micro-managing Cameron's behavior and couldn't find a way to be kind and loving no matter which approach we tried. Our son was a bully – yelling, hitting, running from one mischievous endeavor to another. He had us chasing at his heels. It sounds as if we are fools, but we're not. We just simply didn't know how to get him to cooperate. I was in a nightmare looking for a way out.

I bought *Transforming the Difficult Child* because the title had a promise of kindness and transformation, which I thought was too good to even hope for. I read it over the next couple of weeks and started to lay down a blanket of trust with my son. Almost immediately I saw a change.

Cameron seemed almost dazed by the immediate shift in my response: not getting angry or punitive with him. Initially, he almost seemed deflated that he wasn't getting the same big, upset reactions. At one point, when he was not doing what we asked him to, he literally asked us to force him to do what we requested. When I told him we weren't going to do that anymore, he seemed to accept it, but clearly missed the old dynamic of struggle. When he seemed to be bringing attention to his misbehavior, I told Cameron: "It's my job to see you and to notice the things that are wrong, to make them better. But isn't it better to notice the things you do well?"

I went through every step outlined in the book. The "no warnings before time-outs" was a virtual lifesaver! It has kept my home in peace and harmony. Now, Cameron often runs to take a time-out when I calmly ask him to go. I can then congratulate him for doing such a great job taking his time-out. We all learned tools we need to govern our lives in a peaceful and strong way. About six weeks into the Nurtured Heart strategies, we started the credit system and the difference was astonishing. I now like myself again and feel a deepening bond of trust with my son that was not there before. He is proud and more confident and his kind nature is coming to the surface. Thank you, thank you, thank you.

It is now one year later. Cameron is almost eight, and my husband and I have kept the credit system in place virtually the entire time except for a few weeks' hiatus over the summer (we could really see the difference and went right back to it when school started). Our credit system has evolved over time, depending on what we need to work on as a family, such as 'team work.' Even though Cameron's core aggressive personality hasn't changed, he has had many breakthroughs. It has given us a kind, workable structure to function within and gives our son lots of real successes each day to feel good about. The Nurtured Heart Approach is still an integral part of our family life and probably will be for years to come!

Our anonymous author is a devoted mom who writes, produces and performs music for children in a national touring group.

———————————————— ✿ ————————————————

When we began collecting success stories for this volume, I had the pleasure of an inspiring, in-depth phone interview with this relentlessly dedicated mother. She has been taken down a new path of parental fortitude in service of her high-energy son, their relationship and family peace. This new territory so matches the high amount of positive light this mother emanates in her musical work world.

Knowing that punitive approaches don't feel right or work is just half the battle. Her courageous refusal to continue the dynamic of struggle and refusal to maintain the negative status quo enabled the whole family to find and cultivate a new path beyond the punitive and negative. And Cameron's reaction to this new, benevolent structure was immediate!

What a shift occurred when she 'laid the blanket of trust' with him through nurturing recognitions and a refusal to connect with negatives. It opened up new territory for the whole family and continues to promote within Cameron his innate strengths and gifts.

Thank you, musical mother, for singing the song that nourishes the gentle and strong heart within. It is the song that calls our kind nature forth to the surface. JLE

The sweet irony time and time again is that starting with a refusal to energize negativity and then moving solidly to the new world of appreciation, recognition and acknowledgement brings forth a new and welcome reality. In that reality, there's very little negativity and so much more naturally occurring positivity to respond to – there for the taking. A much better beat to dance to! HNG

Settling the Cheshire Cat Boy

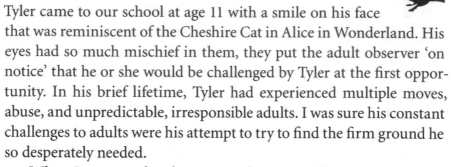

By Dawn Duncan-Lewis

Tyler came to our school at age 11 with a smile on his face that was reminiscent of the Cheshire Cat in Alice in Wonderland. His eyes had so much mischief in them, they put the adult observer 'on notice' that he or she would be challenged by Tyler at the first opportunity. In his brief lifetime, Tyler had experienced multiple moves, abuse, and unpredictable, irresponsible adults. I was sure his constant challenges to adults were his attempt to try to find the firm ground he so desperately needed.

When I went to the elementary classroom of this special needs school to pick up Tyler and two of his classmates for social skills group, I asked them to get into a line. This was an unusual request in our school, but I thought, "What the heck? Let's see what happens. It's a life skill."

The other two students, excited about going to social skills group, walked in a straight line right behind me. Tyler, on the other hand, wagged the tail of the line with his body bouncing off the walls, back and forth from left to right, that familiar smile beaming on his face bigger than ever.

Rather than trying to get Tyler to comply with my request, I decided to turn the moment into a 'Kodak.' I said (with a smile that matched his), "Look at you, going back and forth. I can always count on you to push the envelope, can't I Tyler?" And I laughed as though we shared a joke. He calmed down, quit hitting the walls and walked calmly into the room (that smile still on his face).

I asked the students to get a rug square and to sit in a circle around me. The other two students got their rugs and found a place next to me. Tyler wandered around the room aimlessly, his back to me, seeming to be waiting for a response. I quickly thought, "Okay, don't give energy to this, but make a structure." So I said to the students next to me, "I have several activities planned for us today. We are going to dive right in, and when Tyler is ready, he can join us." Tyler turned around, got a rug square, put it by his classmates' squares, and sat down.

I acknowledged Tyler's presence by saying, "So glad you joined us, Tyler," and continued with the discussion of our agenda. Within a few minutes, Tyler was up again, his back to me, walking aimlessly. I ignored him. As we moved to the next activity, I repeated, "And when Tyler is ready, he can join us." Tyler came over and sat down again. We had to do this one more time before Tyler would settle in with us for good that day, but he finally did.

I found that Tyler needed to walk through this ritual at the beginning of each group session (and usually for every transition from one activity to another), but it began taking less time for him to respond and to finally decide to join us. I learned over time that being with and trusting adults was very difficult for Tyler. I think the combination of not giving energy to his negativity while also setting limits, giving him structure and verbalizing gentle Kodak Moments for joining us seemed to make it safe for him to be with us.

Dawn demonstrates for us the simple magnitude of choosing not to energize the negative but instead recognizing Tyler's deeper need to be seen and accepted within his own trust timeline. She is masterful at picking her battles for compliance – ignoring the minor misbehaviors while bringing in necessary structure and expectations with gentleness and patience. This is all in service of her relationship with Jacob, and it is worth it! Such therapeutic nuances prove to be hinges for more compliance, connection and growth as Jacob responds to Dawn's Recognitions for his baby steps of 'doing' versus negative attention for what he's not doing. Another gem from Dawn! JLE

Disguised in this simple story is the warrior stance of a brilliant clinician refusing to put fuel on the fire of negativity. By so doing, she is fighting for this child's life, opening the door for a new perception on his part of how he will ultimately come to see himself. As long as he remains locked into negativity as a prime mode for gaining connection, he will replicate that wherever he goes, including in his relationship with himself. Dawn is brilliantly loosening his grip on negativity, one finger at a time

– and it is indeed happening. Once this is accomplished, there is truly room for the main event – a transformation to seeing and experiencing himself in a positive way. HNG

Standing at the Summit of Success

By Ellen Thomas

"I hate this school! I'm just gonna leave out!" As expected, my first test came early in the year. He was a rough student, most likely involved in gang activity. He's probably passed all his initiation tests, the "whoopins" from older members of the gang. Uncles, cousins, and brothers have made him their own. In his 14 years, he had seen more hardship and persecution than I will see in my lifetime. His hands carry the wear and worry of a grown man and are only the tip of the iceberg. Inside, I imagine thick aching thorns. Probably all he knew how to do was fight. And when that doesn't work, fight harder.

Like others, he is fluent in the language of confrontation. And today, speaking that language got him a full-day assignment to In-School Success (ISS) – formerly In-School Suspension. He arrives rough and tough, but maybe scared, too. Determined to make an alpha statement, he enters the room striding smoothly, holding his sagging jeans with one hand while carrying his books with the other. He wants me to fear him, I think. I could fear him, I suppose. Instead, I notice that he has recently crusted tears in his eyes. He throws his books onto a desk. "I hate this *%$@ school!" His hand lets go of his jeans just long enough to slam his young rough fist into the door. I startle in surprise; not out of fear, but because I am amazed that my door remained intact. "I'm just gonna leave out! I swear I'm gonna leave out!"

I may be new at this ISS thing, but I am sure that now is <u>not</u> the time to "tell" him that he is not going to leave and that he is going to sit right down and apologize for hitting the door. No way.

He says a few more times that he is "gonna leave out." The third time, as he is making his proclamation, he sits down. Again his hand lets go of his jeans. This time it is because he bites his nails. Cool strider, gang leader, 'grown' man. Worrier, nail biter, child.

Now that he is quiet, it's my turn. I call him by his name and say, "If you are leaving, I'll need to write you a pass. Y'know, paperwork and everything." He looks at me with wide eyes. I continue. "Before you go, though, I want to ask you a couple of questions. Did you come here to get yelled at? Did you come here to have me tell you how bad you are? Did you come here for me to point out all your faults?" "Hell no," he responds, but looking at me with wider, more trusting eyes.

And then I feel the words sliding right out of my mouth. "Well, whew! What a relief! If you had come here for that, I was going to have to tell you that you are in the wrong room! Turns out you're in the right place after all!" He stops biting his nails, smiles, gets out his class work, book, pencil and says, "Will you help me with this?"

"You are certainly in the right place. Of course I will help. I love how much maturity you are showing right now. You must have instinctively realized that staying here was the best choice possible. What strong integrity you have! How awesome this is going to be to see some instant success!"

And so we sat together in the ISS room, quietly working on mean, median, and mode. (I had hoped it wouldn't be math, but I had given a promise.) We took turns looking at the examples and eventually wound up with a page of legitimate-looking work, all before lunch.

This story is so powerful for several reasons. First and foremost was Ellen's great presence of mind in resolutely deciding not to energize this child's negativity. She wisely saw the situation for what it was, refused to let fear dictate her thoughts and actions, and stood fast in choosing not to fall into that trap. Applause!

Then she made another great choice. She chose to create success for this young man at the first available opportunity. And it wasn't just any success, it was deliberate and powerful in delivery and impact. She told him about his greatness in the absolute truth of the moment in a way that I believe he could hear at a heart and soul level. The heart and soul always recognize the truth as far as I can tell, and the impact seems to reverberate in a most meaningful way.

And the other wonderful thing in this story is that, by connecting so powerfully, she has taken a major step on a journey to change this teen's life, clearly a person who could be a lost soul. In a school such as Ellen's where students are surrounded by such appreciation, children start to feel believed in for all the right reasons.

The local newspaper where I live in Tucson once came out with a special section of stories of young adults who had risen out of the ashes of crime and despair to new and positive lifestyles. In each and every incredible story, there was at least one person who really showed up for this young person in trouble and somehow, someway, communicated that he or she truly believed in him. This is what Ellen Thomas does so beautifully in this story. **HNG**

Ellen gives us her 'Zen Slap' Nurtured Heart Approach in a way that injects emotional nutrients under the radar of a young man who is perhaps on the precipice of heart-hardened disaster. She proves that standing with resolve to create and capitalize on the minute moments of positivity is the path to creating yet more positives as well as to forging trust in the moment. The courage and inspirational resolve Ellen offers those in the educational and cultural battlefields remind us that the line to success from failure is sometimes a fine one – and one that can be created in each moment. **JLE**

Turtle Power Forever: Our Amazing Donna-Belle

By Brenda Shepherd-Campbell

Just over three years ago, we were ready to place Donna-Belle in residential care. I was black-and-blue from her physical abuse and afraid of her and for her. She was physically destroying her room, had ripped two doors off the hinges and required up to 20 hours a week of physical restraint to keep herself or others safe. Both therapists working with our family, as well as our pediatric psychiatrist, recommended out-of-home placement for our daughter due to a pattern of escalating physical aggression and suicidal and homicidal statements.

I remember these very dark and desperate days and how many labels and diagnoses were applied. At first, the labels were reassuring, empowering – like now we know what it is, what she needs and what to do. But the more names we heard, the less empowered we felt.

Despite a medicine regime that seemed it would half fill a 5-gallon bucket, the pediatrician was recommending more. At one point, there were 27 or 28 pills a day, including her nutraceuticals. Initially, Concerta® seemed to help Donna-Belle's ADD, but over time we realized in horror that she had lost 23 pounds. I could count her ribs. At one point, she was only sleeping about 40 minutes a day, and later, on another medication, she slept 20 hours a day. There were days Donna-Belle would literally sleep with her head on her desk all day at school. She was on a pill to attend, one to sleep, one for appetite, one for depression and anxiety, and even an anti-psychotic.

I was working full time, going to school as well, and ruthlessly combing the Internet, sometimes 40 hours a week, looking for help. I discovered the Nurtured Heart Approach on a message board for parents, and the description given of a difficult child was our Donna-Belle, exactly! Howard Glasser had an upcoming workshop on the Nurtured Heart Approach in Tucson and an opening for a case study for the workshop. We jumped at this last ditch chance!

Donna-Belle and I and my partner Jan headed for the workshop the day after Donna-Belle turned eight, and we told her that going to Tucson to meet Howard Glasser and learn his approach was our birthday present to her. "We are hoping to give you your life back," we told Donna-Belle, after already discussing with her the possibility she might have to live someplace else. (At the workshop, Donna-Belle was on her best behavior, very shy and refusing to disobey, not exactly what Howard had in mind as a case study to demonstrate consequences to the audience. He finally found an opportunity to demonstrate a time-out without need for physical restraint.)

I remember reading Glasser's book *Transforming the Difficult Child* while on a trip to look for a new home for the family in the Spokane area of Washington. It was 3 a.m. when I had an epiphany in understanding how therapy can actually make things worse for some difficult children. As Howard said, for a child who already has the impression that she gets more energy and relationship through adversity, talking about problems deepens that very impression. And so much of Donna-Belle's treatment was primarily and resoundingly focused on problems.

We had a therapist for Donna-Belle, plus an on-call, in-home family therapist who could come anytime, 24 hours a day. Therapists were our version of life support, like an IV, or oxygen; so the thought of letting go of this was really scary. When we finally did, Donna-Belle began to thrive; it was amazing to see this. It was like watching a flower bloom on high-speed film.

The same thing ultimately occurred with the medication. After beginning Glasser's approach and realizing our daughter did not seem to be present anymore, we made another dramatic decision to discontinue the medication, which was against medical advice. Not only did we decide we could handle Donna-Belle off medication once we started seeing results from the Nurtured Heart Approach, but this powerful stance also empowered Donna-Belle rather than the medications to be the one in control of her behavior.

She loves Teenage Mutant Ninja Turtles, so we started applying the Nurtured Heart Approach by talking to Donna-Belle about using her 'Turtle Power.' We said, "You have these turtle powers inside of you and you are using them to stay in control." Within six weeks of using the approach as if our and Donna-Belle's lives depended on it, there was no more evidence of physical aggression.

We did Positive Recognitions, but we called our version 'Positive Dive Bombing.' We literally barraged her with the positives she was showing us. At first, she didn't like the positives or compliments at all. She'd yell back in a rage, "I'm NOT using my mind well! I'm NOT using my Teenage Mutant Ninja Power!" But we kept it up anyway.

For the Credit System, Howard coined the term 'Donna-Belle Dollars' and she earned a whopping $375 the first day! On another day, Donna-Belle was on fire with positive behaviors – breaking the bank at $2000! Needless to say, we had to restructure things a bit to accommodate Donna-Belle's success and our pocket!

Now, Donna-Belle is thriving at school and home and she is medication-free. She has gone from using her great power and energy in dance classes to studying karate. In less than a year's time, 'Miss Turtle Power' has gone from white belt to yellow belt in rank, no small feat. She is also functioning well in a regular classroom of over 25 students.

She accepts everyone and is willing to be a friend regardless of what the 'in' crowd may think about someone. I think this makes her one of the most amazing people I know, and I tell her on a very regular basis how much I try to be like HER! She tells me that I am weird, but that is how kids SHOULD think of their parents!

Donna-Belle was just tested for problems at school in math and written language and will be receiving an IEP (Individual Education Plan) for these issues. Rather than feeling like a failure and shutting down, she sees this as an empowering and exciting development. She has been diagnosed with Asperger's Syndrome, which is a type of high-functioning Autism where the primary problem, for her at least, is the reading of nonverbal cues. We are working with her and continuing to use the Nurtured Heart Approach to help reinforce all the wonderful positive successes she has.

When we decided to foster an infant in our home, Donna-Belle requested that the baby's crib be in her room. She's also been able to speak of her fears of losing time and attention to the baby, which is a great sign of emotional and social skill development. We now have two foster children, ages 16 months and 2½ years. Donna-Belle is struggling with the oldest one but she is able to verbally share her feelings with us and has not acted out in a physical way with any anger at all. She is very excited at the prospect of our adopting both of the babies in the near future. Donna-Belle is an amazing big sister.

The day after her birthday each year, we celebrate Donna-Belle's 're-birthday,' commemorating the day we found the Nurtured Heart Approach! This year, we will celebrate Donna-Belle's fourth 're-birthday.' She is now 11½ and is such an amazing young lady. She has been 'caught' using Howie's methods with her foster sister when the little one is behaving in a way that Donna-Belle finds inappropriate. She is doing so much better than we could ever have imagined or hoped for! As her brother Dalton-Michael begins to enter the 'terrible twos,' she will be able to draw on all the resources she has learned with the Nurtured Heart Approach to have even greater successes!

I hope that I can help other parents discover the sanity that lies within the structure of the Nurtured Heart Approach. Without it, I really think our family would have self-destructed. Now we are growing and thriving and loving life!

Brenda has worked with children for over 30 years, from neighborhood babysitter to full-time nanny and everything in between. She is also a Massage Therapist, a Phlebotomist, a Registered Nursing Assistant and a foster mom. Her partner and co-parent Jan is working toward her Bachelor's Degree in Criminal Justice. Despite not being a parent or even having much exposure to young children prior to joining the family, Jan has been an amazing step-parent, dedicated to finding whatever was needed to help Donna-Belle. Jan has decided to legally adopt Donna-Belle and in doing so has given their daughter a feeling of permanency of family that she had not even been able to articulate her need for until after she experienced it. Brenda and Jan have requested to be part of a message board for parents who are working with the Nurtured Heart Approach as a means of mutual support.

This is perhaps the most moving and inspiring of all our stories for me. Jan, Brenda and the amazing Donna-Belle's passage through the dark times of over-medication, therapists galore and possible relinquishment speaks to how hard it can really be before a new gate opens and offers hope and a literal re-birthday.

What heroines these three are! In the midst of such hopelessness, Brenda finds her ailing family a venue for deep hope and complete transformation. It is no easy road to realize that therapy is making things worse and that you'll need to release your own version of life support in service of a new life raft that you steer by yourself into uncharted waters.

This is exactly what Jan and Brenda did, and with the Nurtured Heart master himself! I love that they created their own versions of the approach. Turtle Power Recognitions, Donna-Belle Dollars and Positive Dive-Bombing became their new arsenal, applying the approach 'like their lives depended upon it.' It is clear all their lives did depend upon that deep resolve and refusal to stay with a problem-focused system of treatment. You are the true masters of your new life, committed mamas! And to the amazing Donna-Belle, 'Miss Turtle Power' and 'Big Sister Extraordinaire:' you truly ARE AMAZING! JLE

I had the honor of meeting this child and these loving parents. I also had the daunting task of making some very strange recommendations that required trusting my intuition and using all my personal power in order to have the courage to say what I did.

I could tell that, although this child was receiving a wealth of therapy when we first met, which is normally assumed to be good, every bit of it was actually further rewarding this child for negativity. And this was the very last thing Donna-Belle needed because she already believed to the 'Nth' degree that intense, connected and juicy relationship and intimacy were best gotten through adversity. Although I'm sure that all the therapists would deny this, they were essentially talking to this child about her problems. And Donna-Belle, being a brilliant observer of "what IS," realized that problems were the way to guarantee that the caring and energized relationships would continue to thrive. This, of course, is not the best kind of relationship and will eventually and always backfire.

Therefore, my recommendations were to fire the therapists and to fire the pediatric psychiatrist, supposedly the very best in the region, because they obviously had no idea what they were doing. That's a tough call for a family that's faced with a very aggressive child who was falling apart at the seams.

But the great news is that these parents fully understood their dilemma, fully understood that the Nurtured Heart Approach would work, and fully understood my instructions to undertake it as if their life depended upon it. By refusing to energize negativity, they literally broke their daughter's addiction, and by refusing to NOT energize success, they pulled her into a new way of living her life. Once she saw that the other door was closed for good and this new door was wide open, she decided to use her intensity in wonderful and great ways!

Not responding to negativity was made much easier by this approach's way of doing consequences that finally worked. It does so by eliminating warnings (which only give relationship and energy for negativity), by having a mindset of being unceremonious – an aspect that totally helps, too, in not giving energy to the problem – and by viewing the end of the consequence as the way to purposefully move on to the next round of successes, a part of the process that served this child and these parents so well.

This all was a tall order for Brenda and Jan, and I give them all the credit. These parents are my definition of a hero and they have produced another hero – Donna-Belle. Congratulations to this great and growing family and Happy Re-Birthday to you all! HNG

SECTION III:
THE PERFECT CONSEQUENCES

Having an effective way to enact consequences is a hugely important aspect of the Nurtured Heart Approach. Even though a great deal can be accomplished by taking the stands of energizing positivity and refusing to energize negativity, many challenging children can only realize the full-blown transformation – the shift to using their intensity in new and wonderful ways – when they come to see the exacting clarity of limits and the results of exceeding those limits; and ultimately come to feel like they don't want to waste time breaking rules any longer. The attraction dissolves when they see that there's no more energy to be garnered for negativity – all the energy, relationship and passionate connection are only available through successfulness.

In the 10 years since *Transforming the Difficult Child* was published, I have continued to simplify the Nurtured Heart Approach's philosophy on how to best accomplish clear consequences. In the beginning, we recommended that the child fulfill consequences by actually taking a time-out in a chair. We came to see, however, that time-out is more a function of the child perceiving that she has had a result of breaking a rule and that the consequence need not take the shape of a particular method or appearance.

Fewer adults using this approach insist that the consequence happen in a chair. Instead, they find it is perfectly sufficient to create the illusion that the cycle (consequence) is complete just by declaring a momentary 'reset,' turning away and back, even seconds later, and declaring that the consequence was done successfully and the child is now "back in the game." And many parents and teachers use various other names to describe a consequence or time-out, such as reset, recess, pause or take a break.

The new point of view is that the 'awakening' doesn't happen as a result of the harshness or length of the consequence, but rather from the child 'awakening to' the greatness within himself.

In this refined view, the consequence is really just a momentary break designed to be over quickly and just as quickly lead the child to glimpse who she really is – a child who is indeed now NOT breaking the rules and making other choices of greatness.

The Nurtured Heart Approach is thus all about leading the child – by way of first-hand experiences and by way of how we choose to see things – to further iterations of the qualities of greatness that he already possesses but had previous been unaware of.

One cannot enact successful consequences without also having great faith: faith that the child is capable of handling the result of her actions, faith that the child has the inner wisdom to process the lessons inherent in the approach, faith that the child can recover, and faith in the child's inner strength and innate resiliency. Limits and consequences also require faith that your child will ultimately come to love you on deeper and deeper levels despite your efforts to hold them accountable.

Getting out of the way and allowing children the freedom to break the rules as the way to see the results is an ultimate expression of faith, similar to the faith God has in us: allowing us the freedom to make choices, break rules, and experience the results, if we so desire. For parents, the challenge of setting clear limits and consequences is an expression of faith in your child's ability to use great judgment and make great decisions. It is not our job to stop our children from breaking rules. It's our job to have faith that it is their job and faith that they CAN. Here are some stories that demonstrate that leap of faith taken to make consequences work.

Howard Glasser

Pause and Play

By Stephen Crippen

Five-year-old Alex was brought to therapy by his mother, Sheri, to work on troubling behaviors that he was presenting in his pre-school. In Sheri's words, "The school would call and tell me what he was doing, and I couldn't believe they were talking about my son." He had been provoking other children and disrupting the class quite often, even though his behaviors at home were very good.

In the therapy room, Alex was a delightful (and sometimes exhausting!) ball of energy who smiled often and gave us plenty of opportunities to practice time-outs, Kodak Moment, and other Nurtured Heart techniques. We talked about how highly energetic Alex is and how some schools just have a hard time handling intense kids well. Sheri said that, just before coming in to see me, she had moved Alex to another pre-school and his behaviors got much better. Nevertheless, she wanted to improve her own understanding of her son's highly active personality and also be sure he continued to function well in pre-school.

In one session, we practiced time-outs, and by the end of the session his mother felt that she had gotten the hang of it. We discussed how time-outs are more effective – and less likely to backfire – when they're kept nice and short. Sheri decided to use 'red light' to indicate a time-out and 'green light' when the time-out is over to avoid the negative perceptions that the former 'time-outs' held for both Alex and her. We practiced 'red light, green light' and mom felt encouraged about the new approach.

When they returned the next week, Sheri reported that the new time-outs were working really well, but that Alex himself had suggested a change – a change that made a world of difference. Alex told her he would rather she say 'pause' and 'play' than red and green light. Sheri explained, "He got the idea from the TV remote control. When you press 'pause,' everything freezes. When you press 'play,' everything starts moving again." We practiced a time-out using the words 'pause' and 'play.' When Sheri said 'pause,' Alex froze in mid-motion, his eyes alight. Then when Sheri said 'play,' he started moving again.

"He made it fun," Sheri said. The time-outs were going very well, both at home and at school, and there hadn't been any complaints about Alex's behavior.

Alex is a fortunate child: he has a mother who welcomes his contribution to solutions. By embracing his suggestion about the time-outs, Sheri nurtured him on two levels: she began giving him effective time-outs that didn't squelch his natural energy, and her use of his 'pause and play' idea was itself a Kodak Moment, an opportunity to nurture his delightful creativity and imagination.

Stephen Crippen is a Certified Nurtured Heart Specialist and Psychotherapist who works in Seattle with adolescents and parents to help people of all ages live, work, and relate more joyfully.

———————————— ♡ ————————————

Stephen's story is a perfect example of the energetic shift from intense to cooperative behavior achieved by guiding a bright light like Alex without dampening his flame. His mother's wisdom in following her wildly delightful son's own creative version of consequences is the cherry on top. That wise and workable alliance clearly was a sustaining foundation for preserving and nourishing the heart of the relationship. And it worked!

Thank you, Stephen, for offering this gem and for walking the healing path to support parents in becoming empowered healers in their own right. JLE

It is so much fun to read Stephen's story and the creative journey of this mother who used the initial crisis to create a new trajectory of success for her son and for their relationship.

What Stephen left out in his modesty is something I came to quickly realize about his greatness. When he studied for his advanced training in the Nurtured Heart Approach, he was the guy who so got it at a core level that within minutes he was reinventing and evolving yet greater versions. My favorites were a series of e-mails I received about how he would 'smart bomb' the children he worked with – code for his relentless and powerful version of confronting children with their successfulness. I love the freedom Stephen extends to parents and teachers and the freedom he takes in creating such joyful iterations of this approach.

I believe it is a great gift to find just the right way to make all aspects of this approach work with a particular child and a particular situation. I applaud the mother's great creativity in finding a consequence that circumvented the recollections of strained time-outs of the past and that served to put a new and lighter frame to moving through the consequences and on to the 'smart bombs.' *HNG*

———————————— ⟨♥⟩ ————————————

A Grandmother's Postscript: Jumping on the Bed

By Brenda Murphy

My two young granddaughters were nearly age 3 at the time of this story and have had their hearts nurtured from birth. They are the closest of cousins, born at practically the same time! The story begins on a day they decided to jump on the guest bed. This is not acceptable. They know that when I say "Unacceptable" or "No ma'am," they need to s-t-o-p. Even at this tender age, they get it. When a rule is broken, 'Mamie' (that's me) hands down a consequence in 10 seconds or less.

I heard them giggling and I heard the jumping. I walked to the door of the guest room and said nothing. I simply stood there and made eye contact with them. Leigh abruptly stopped. Bailey stopped after one more jump. Leigh looked at Bailey and said, "Uh, oh. We broke a rule. I'm going to sit in the chair and think about a better choice next time. Right, Mamie?" I nearly exploded into laughter, but I know better. "Leigh, that is an excellent choice for a big girl like you. I am proud of your decision." Leigh goes to the chair. She sits there for about 30 seconds, jumps up, and runs to tell me she's sorry and won't do that again. In the meantime, Bailey is watching all of this interaction, still on the bed. Bailey dismounts, gets in the chair, sits about 10 seconds, yells "Me, too!" and flies out of the chair to apologize and get her hug and 'welcome back.' Having observed Leigh, I think Bailey just decided to stick with a winning formula with a "Me, too!" The girls haven't jumped on the bed since. Nurtured Heart works. And I have two baby grandsons who will likewise be the beneficiaries of the Nurtured Heart Approach.

I love Brenda's light but absolutely clear touch in depicting the consequences in this story. She's absolutely clear the girls earned a consequence — even a little bit of jumping on the bed was breaking the rule — and I love how clear she was in knowing her intention to get right back to lovingly appreciating her granddaughters.

*What a gift her light and playful style is to all involved. Thank you, Brenda, for sharing this. **HNG***

Somehow I'm not surprised that such a fabulous firecracker of a grandmother would have such energetic granddaughters! Brenda shares her wealth here – meeting Leigh and Bailey's exuberant bed jumping with equal resolve and intention to shift the energy. She shows us the potency of reset energy backed by a heart of benevolent firmness – all the deep roots of a perfect consequence!

*In this case, the rules were so crystal clear, only Grandmother's glance was required and Leigh knew the drill. With Leigh's seamless shift via practiced resets, Bailey is pulled irresistibly into the stream of self-reset success as well. This non-punitive consequence offers both jumpers a new leap into greatness and appreciation – for the better choice to stop and reset their high energy (rather than feeling like bad girls for a rule break). Brenda's magnanimous recognition (welcoming the girls back post-reset) affirms new possibilities created by the reset – the newest moment of better choices! Thank you to our wise Georgia Queen, Brenda. Supporting those small, esteemed leaps in the right direction offers so much for our future jumpers! **JLE***

Sarah's Story

By Sarah Johnson

As a mother of two boys, one of whom is very energetic, I had read several books about discipline and behavior problems. I grew up with conservative values, based on a Christian upbringing, and was spanked myself as a child. After reading one book that advocated controlled, calm spanking as a consequence for misbehavior, I thought spanking was the normal progression in discipline. I felt I was doing the right thing but it did not seem to work. I then read another book, *Smart Discipline,* and put it into practice. At first it worked, but after a couple of weeks it slowly began to lose steam because it was hard to keep up with and maintain consistency. I was at a loss and began to think that there was nothing out there that I could use to help my child.

I felt like I was falling deeper into a bottomless well with my 4-year-old son, Jacob. His difficulties with changes in routine, and screaming "stupid" when frustrated, had escalated to hitting and spitting. After he was kicked out of two 'Mother's Day Out' programs, I began to suspect there was something going on that was bigger than just average behavior problems, but I still had no solution. I was slowly coming to my wit's end.

Then the therapist who was in the process of evaluating Jacob recommended the book *Transforming the Difficult Child: The Nurtured Heart Approach.* Once I got the book, I simply could not put it down. I literally read it cover to cover. The reason I found it so intriguing was that the concept made so much sense. Immediately, I put it into practice, and within three days, the difference was like night and day. I was amazed at the transformation!

There was no need to spank now; the whole concept of quick time-outs worked so much better! I keep my authority, stay calm and it stops the problem behavior! The biggest challenge is learning to change the way I speak to the children – to speak to them from a positive lens rather than nagging them, criticizing or lecturing. The boys just love to remind me about time-outs that I need to take once in awhile for myself if I forget and raise my voice!

My husband is now seeing and recognizing what the boys do well instead of focusing on all their mistakes or bad choices. He is learning how to give Positive Recognitions, and the boys actually comment on it when he notices what they do well. This approach meets my children's basic need for attention by recognizing their good behavior instead of waiting for the bad. Because my husband and I have learned to become a united force by putting into practice the Nurtured Heart Approach, it has made all the difference in the world in our family life. They no longer try to set one parent against the other in opposition. It just does not work for them any more. With the boundaries clearly set, both our children know what to expect.

Because Jacob was able to receive the nurturing he needed, I began to notice how much more at peace he was with his brother Christian, with his dad, with me and with life in general. This was a breath of fresh air. Where there was once chaos, peace and tranquility began to take over. (Once Jacob's evaluation was complete, there was still not a formal diagnosis even though he showed characteristics consistent with Asperger's Syndrome.)

I honestly believe that the concepts of the short time-out and community service when needed were the most effective instruments in bringing control back to us as parents during this difficult period. With the boundaries clearly set, both our children know what to expect.

When I began to implement the credit system, my 8-year-old son, Christian, really liked the fact that he was receiving recognition for his efforts. On one occasion I asked him to help set the table and he asked, "Do I receive more credits for doing it?" With the most energetic and excited voice I had, I said, "Of course, you do!" It was written all over his face that he was quite pleased with himself. Jacob did not find it so appealing; however, I will continue to praise him and provide positive reinforcement.

Because I believe so strongly in the Nurtured Heart Approach, I plan to teach it to other parents in our church through a parenting class. I believe this information is too important not to share with every parent, grandparent or caretaker. I am so thankful for this awesome book. I share it with everyone. If I had a pile of Howard's books at the grocery store, I'd just be handing them out like candy to everyone, especially those parents that I see who are struggling. Thank you for your devotion in writing this much-needed material. It has made an enormous difference in the life of my family.

Sarah Johnson, happily married to a wonderful man for 14 years, has two beautiful boys who keep her quite busy. She currently attends Southeastern University in Hammond, Louisiana, deciding to return to school after 20 years to "help others who may be in the same situation as I was." Sarah owns a successful in-home sales business, which helps her find enjoyment and friendship. Sarah shares her philosophy: "Taking pleasure in something I find worthwhile helps me be a better wife and mother. I am a very busy person, but believe in living each moment to the fullest."

Blessings and applause to this dedicated mother! She was trying so hard to be a good mother, realizing that spanking wasn't working. It takes a lot of courage and fortitude to give up lectures, nagging and spanking, but what rewards to do so! Despite what we may have grown up with, negativism and punishment circumvent inner successes, and ultimately outer successes, if they are not connected with self-pride and genuine self-esteem.

Sarah and her husband shifted the whole family dynamic through Recognitions, Appreciations and Credits as the nourishing and critical foundation, thus allowing short time-outs to really work! Jacob and Christian now have the benefit of consequences that don't impart inner weakness or failure. They are blessed with parents who have keys to unlock the doors of success and share them with others! Much gratitude to Sarah and her family for sharing their success! JLE

For many parents, making the leap from either conventional or faith-based parenting, or both, is a major step in life. It is not just an incidental decision. However, when faced with a crisis of having nothing work with a child and escalating negativity, push can come to shove very quickly. Still, making such a change can bring up a lot of fears and concerns.

Great credit here goes to Sarah and her husband for letting the needs of their family and children direct them in searching for what else might help. Not everyone, even in such a demanding situation, would have remained open to such major change.

The Johnsons did many things that made the new consequences work. It would not have worked if they hadn't fully adopted their new intention of showering the children with recognition and appreciation and without their concerted effort to no longer give energy and relationship to negativity. So it wasn't just changing the consequences that made the difference.

However, in reading a story such as this, it always reminds me that corporal punishments hold to an underlying precept or belief that the stronger the consequence, the greater the impact. Many parents facing challenging behaviors wind up escalating the magnitude of the spankings, thinking that they surely need to play hardball, and if only they could find just the right level of spanking or yelling or both, the child will finally awaken to being afraid to break the rules again.

The problem is that the fear and hurt engendered in these kinds of consequences wind up really hurting the parent-child relationship. And they really seem to hurt the soul of both the parent and the child. The evidence now is overwhelming that children who are spanked have significantly greater incidences of depression, anxiety, substance abuse, and a host of other lingering and related issues.

The irony is that our society largely believes that making a consequence more drastic or punitive will create the desired outcome. But the evidence now seems to support that the Nurtured Heart Approach's amazingly simple way of offering a consequence – barely entailing anything beyond a few seconds of the child's time – gives the child a greater sense of result and is a much more effective way of playing hardball.

Maybe real hardball is in refusing to give energy to negativity; and maybe the other aspect of real hardball is in refusing NOT to give lots of notification of success. Combining these with a delightful and light way of saying, when needed, "that's a broken rule – reset," turns out to be way more effective and powerful than what so many of us were exposed to as kids – harsh punishments.

And so many of us wish our parents would have found an alternative with a lighter touch, rather than continuing endlessly to find the next harshest punishment that didn't stand a chance of working. Congratulations to the Johnson family for finding the lighter touch and for their brilliant efforts in making all the pieces come together. HNG

———————————— ⟨♡⟩ ————————————

Lowering the Rope

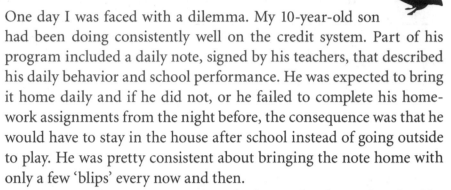

By Lisa Bravo

One day I was faced with a dilemma. My 10-year-old son had been doing consistently well on the credit system. Part of his program included a daily note, signed by his teachers, that described his daily behavior and school performance. He was expected to bring it home daily and if he did not, or he failed to complete his homework assignments from the night before, the consequence was that he would have to stay in the house after school instead of going outside to play. He was pretty consistent about bringing the note home with only a few 'blips' every now and then.

It was Halloween morning, and Christopher began his day like every other. His pirate costume had been laid out on the living room floor for two days in anticipation of the big event. I suppressed the urge to remind him about making sure he had everything he needed for school and to bring his note home. He was well aware that there would be no exceptions even though it was Halloween. At around 10:00 a.m., I received a voicemail from my calm but noticeably stressed-out son stating, "Hi Mom, it's me. I forgot my workbook at home, so I know I have my consequence. That means I can't go trick-or-treating tonight. I really want to go, but I know I have a consequence." With that he hung up. Everything in me wanted to change my mind, give in to him, not be consistent, and essentially look the other way. Close to tears, I called my husband, knowing it was going to be a hard lesson and wondering if we were being too strict about the rule. But it had been going so well and I did not want to jeopardize all the progress we had made. To think that he called me from school to tell on himself! That never would have happened a year ago. My husband, the logical one, said, "A consequence is a consequence, no matter what day it is. He can help pass out candy with me if he can hold it together." In my heart I knew it was the right thing to do, but I felt sad for my little boy.

When he got home from school, Christopher again told me he had forgotten to bring his homework to school. In a last desperate measure, he asked if he could go trick-or-treating. When I said no, he burst into tears and PUT HIMSELF IN TIME-OUT in his room. Within about 15 minutes he had calmed himself down and stopped crying. He came out of his room and calmly and respectfully told me he found a solution: He wanted to use his 'Get out of Jail Free Card' (a part of the credit system designed to give him a chance for successes; i.e., a way to lower the rope in the tank, just like Shamu's trainers had done). He was able to use the 'Get out of Jail Free Card' to forgo one consequence per school year but it could not be used for 'big deal rules' like fighting at school, swearing or hurting others. Also, initiating the use of the card had to be done by him. Because he had had such a good year, he had not yet used his card. VOILA! He had found a way to solve the problem appropriately!

There were many choices he could have made throughout that day, beginning with falling apart at school and having a rotten day. He also chose to be respectful and stay in control when it was clear I was not going to cave-in. In NOT losing it, he was being successful. Because of his accumulated inner wealth, he was able to assess the situation and rely on his own problem-solving abilities to get through to the other side. Through the credit system, we created a structure built on success and healthy problem-solving. Christopher was able to experience profound success within the context of a first-hand experience. A win/win situation for all involved.

What a brilliant example of creative consequences in a family where a strong foundation of clarity and consistency already had been built. Lisa is so right about Christopher's inner wealth and resilience being so strong that he was not only able to share his mistake in truthful integrity, he was able to hold himself together through the angst and problem-solve on his own accord. In this case, the consequence option maintained Christopher's personal integrity and the family's consequence contract without supporting or rewarding negativity. The special yearly option instead became a brilliant support, punctuating Christopher's amazing resourcefulness.

Hats off to Lisa and her husband for not letting Christopher off the hook or diluting Christopher's self-responsibility through reminders, lectures or giving in. This would have precluded the beautiful outcome of Christopher calling on his inner resources and creativity to stand on his own behalf in a balanced way.

Christopher, to you I say: BRILLIANT use of your inner control! Staying in your personal power allowed you to creatively remember a solution that reflects the amazing success that you already are and deserve! JLE

I would love to add to Jennifer's amazing commentary but she said everything I would have said and more. I totally applaud Lisa and family for the brilliance that led to this moment of creative consequence as well the brilliance exercised by all involved as it unfolded. HNG

Transforming the Wildcat Girl

By Jamie Harr and Dawn Duncan-Lewis

Very particular elements need to be present in a child's life in order for him or her to navigate the developmental stages of childhood. For instance, an infant needs to feel 'safe' and to be able to 'trust' that her caregiver will be there to meet her most basic needs, which include comforting when she cries, holding her, giving her food and drink, being playful with her, looking into her eyes and 'seeing' her, talking to her lovingly and gently, and so forth. If these elements are present, there is a very good chance that the child will not only be able to fulfill her first developmental stage, but that she will also be able to launch to the next one.

Most of the children who come to our K-12 school for children with special needs are in what the creators of the developmental assessment we use at our school call Stage II (or 2½ to 5 years old) in the areas of behavior, communication and socialization. [Wood, M.M., Davis, K.R., Swindle, F.H., & Quirk, C.A. (1996). Developmental Therapy-Developmental Teaching (3rd ed.) Austin, TX: ProED.] That means, for some reason (or reasons), these children got stuck developmentally in those areas of growth.

This developmental stagnation can be caused by many things – the child's own inner time-clock, physical or mental illness, stress and crisis (in the child and/or the family), lack of a nurturing caregiver, lack of healthy and effective limit-setting, neglect, abuse, and so on. With time, unsuccessfully navigated stages of development can also be coupled with a significant amount of anger and/or depression. These children tend to be sad and/or frustrated that the ways they have been trying to get their needs met aren't working for them or for the adults in their lives.

The Nurtured Heart Approach has the perfect combination of nurturing elements to remediate developmental delays such as these. Being 'seen' and being made to feel they are valuable persons, coupled with firm limits and structure, are just what the doctor would order for social developmental delays such as the children in our school experience. It is amazing to witness time and again that, when the right elements are provided, growth happens!

Trina, age 10, came to our school in the middle of the school year. She had short dark hair that went in every direction and a 'wild-child' look in her eyes. Trina was, for lack of a better word, "oppositional." If her teacher, Miss J, told her to do something, she would typically go into a tirade, her body would fly out of her desk, and an animal-like growl or angry cat-hiss would emit from her mouth. If Miss J pursued the issue, Trina would throw herself under one of the teacher's desks and, if a pair of adult legs were within reach, a bite on the ankle was likely to occur. Miss J had only been at our school for a few weeks, replacing a teacher on leave, when Trina arrived.

Miss J was pretty challenged to know how to interact with Trina in a way that would produce the desired effect. Quite honestly, the sheer volume and violence of Trina's responses to her environment were unnerving and challenging to the entire school staff to say the least.

That spring, we did a developmental assessment and found that, at age 10, Trina was functioning at Stage II in behavior, communication and socialization. Again, we had a frantic toddler trying to get her needs met in ways that were not working for her or her teacher.

When school started up again in the fall, Trina's new teacher was Mrs. S. The first day of class, it wasn't long before Mrs. S was with Trina on the floor, Trina screaming as loudly as anyone could imagine. Although she was in her first-day-of-school dress, Mrs. S was trying her best to hold Trina to prevent her from following through on her physical threats to bite and kick her. Mrs. S soon realized that, while she was used to being the one in charge, she had indeed met her match! Fortunately for Trina, so had she.

Mrs. S knew that in order to receive Trina's respect, she had her work cut out for her. She realized that IEP (Individual Education Plan) meant just what it said, "individual." So the things that worked with other students were not necessarily going to work with Trina. For instance, Trina did not swear like most of the other students in the class, but she did do that annoying "hisssssing" sound, and then refused to talk at all. If she refused to answer a question or continued making hissing sounds, she was to take a time-out, just the same as a student who swore in class. And as usual when the adults asserted themselves as the leaders, this did not sit well with Trina. When she refused to leave class, she would be escorted out by staff. No one wanted to escort Trina because she was very challenging and would bite and try to trip staff as they walked. At first Trina would take a time-out and come back to class but would refuse to work and would not speak...so out again she and the staff would go and start all over.

We continued to be consistent, however, and it did pay off. Although during the first month of school we still heard lots of screaming from Trina, Mrs. S could tell that she and her staff were moving in the right direction. Trina's outbursts were becoming fewer and she was beginning to show some interest in being relational with her teachers. It took lots of very consistent limit-setting AND Active Recognitions for the teachers in her class to start to have a relationship with Trina. In the beginning, it was very tricky (and sometimes scary) to find ways to 'Kodak' Trina. She could be SO reactive, sometimes staff were afraid to talk to her because they did not know how she would respond. But we tried anyway, noticing a smile, what she was wearing, that she had combed her hair, anything we could think of. Gradually and VERY slowly, she began to talk to us and to use her words, especially when she did not like the way things were going for her. But this was progress!

One of Trina's biggest challenges was the image she had of herself. She was convinced that she couldn't learn. Her statements to Mrs. S the first few weeks of school were, "I don't read!" and "I can't write!" She may have had a tough time reading and writing but she was smart and had a great memory, so her teachers decided to build on those strengths. Mrs. S immediately began an intense reading program with Trina in the mornings. Mornings were Trina's special time with the teacher's assistant, Mrs. B, a very sweet and tender person. Trina loved being with Mrs. B. Trina's reading program was taught in another room, so it didn't matter how 'badly' she read. It was only she and Mrs. B, alone together. Her reading improved greatly and quickly. Writing, however, was still challenging. Even when she was willing to write, she couldn't spell the words. So Mrs. S would pen words for her ('lowering the rope'). Eventually Trina didn't want her teacher to write for her anymore. Academics began to be a great way to praise

Trina because she was having so much success. Anytime her teachers saw Trina doing something academically, they would congratulate her. Eventually she wanted the praise and would work like the dickens!

Trina had greatly improved in other areas as well. Only two months into the school year, Trina had completely stopped hissing and growling and was a champion at using her words. Not only that, she had become a sort of teacher's assistant herself, tutoring her peers in their academics. Suddenly, the rules were very important to her and she was more than willing to not only comply, but to help the other students realize when they needed to follow the rules, too. By using clear and consistent limit-setting, trust building, and lots of reflection, Trina's teachers were able to help her grow and develop.

Mrs. S realized that she had changed as well. She was more inclined to try to see things from her students' points of view. In Trina's case, she was the 'boss' at home and was used to running her own world. Mrs. S let her be a leader and have some ownership in the classroom, so Trina felt more respected and was then more willing to give Mrs. S respect.

By the end of October that school year, we had noticed so many positive changes in Trina that we decided to do another developmental assessment of her. The assessment showed that she had matured TWO STAGES in the seven months since her last assessment. She was now at her chronological age level socially and behaviorally! Trina's teachers could see that she had blossomed into a very nice young lady.

By the end of that school year, Trina had mainstreamed to her neighborhood school in a behavioral program. During the next school year, her teacher there told Mrs. S that Trina was about to go to a general education classroom. Her teacher expressed sadness at the thought of losing her, even though she was very happy for Trina's success. She said Trina would really be missed in her class by the students and staff alike. Our former 'Wildcat Girl' had found new means of channeling her wildness. Trina had found true power and successful ways to positively channel her intensity into academic challenges, self-value and the capacity to lead others.

Jamie D. Harr is a special education teacher at a school for children with emotional and behavioral disorders. She is also a Nurtured Heart consultant. Dawn Duncan-Lewis is a marriage and family therapist who has been working in private practice with children, young adults and parents, in schools since 1999, and for Catholic Community Services since 2003.

This story reminds me that it is so often the most demanding and challenging children who teach us the greatest lessons. I personally am indebted to the toughest kids I have worked with because they invariably got me to resolutely dig my heels in and make the concerted effort to raise the bar of the approach. Thereafter, everyone benefited. And because of the much greater intensity of a child like Trina, the turnarounds are always that much more gratifying, and the outcomes that much greater. I am convinced that the very same intensity that was locked into negativity becomes the force that propels a new life of greatness. And in Trina's case: look out world. She will undoubtedly be a force of greatness to be reckoned with.

Congratulations to Dawn and Jamie and Mrs. S for their great choice to dig in and create ways to get the process started and to continue to raise the trajectory. They demonstrated brilliant and concerted effort, unwillingness to give up, intelligent collaboration and fantastic creativity. These are all wonderful qualities of greatness. HNG

Another gem from Jamie and Dawn, proof that even the most oppositional wildness can be tamed without breaking the wild one's spirit. Proof, also, that even the wildest are especially capable of flourishing with the right blend of consequences grounded and secured by a relationship rooted in trust and meaningful connection. Jamie and Dawn are masters of holding the positive in a hurricane, as well as understanding the use of the approach for developmental support. This story highlights that even the most challenging child can be mainstreamed into the regular classroom with dedicated strength-building and the right consequences! JLE

Meltdown and Time-Out: A Follow-up

By Michele Greenish

This story of meltdown and time-out in the park is one of my favorites. It brings home to me once again how often our intense children truly are our educators. They have their unique way of stretching our parental and often personal endurance to the utmost limits. It seems from what I have observed and from my own experience as parent that we often need to reach such limits before we can put ourselves on the line and learn a whole new pattern of parenting our intense child.

This Mom, Gretchen, had reached such limits and was determined to change things around. Pulling from her newly found Nurtured Heart Approach skills all the strength, fearless determination and wisdom of the heart she could muster, she learned not to feed any reaction in response to 8-year-old Chris' outbursts of anger. She would simply apply the necessary consequences. Getting there is one thing; but staying with it once you got there is a whole other dimension. This Mom was fearlessly determined to hold her ground. Her skills were crucial for the process of healing and transformation that took place over several months, culminating in this episode at the park. The setting is Switzerland, where many families go to the park regularly after school.

By this time, Gretchen recalls, time-out has become easier and easier for Chris to do successfully. Often it is nothing more than a hand gesture from Mom, like on a soccer field. Chris goes and sits on the grass for a few minutes. He usually calms down quickly. Little could she anticipate at this point the dreadful meltdown awaiting at the park on this day.

An older woman arrives at the park with her 2-year-old grandchild. Even though Chris has never met either, she asks Chris to give the toddler a turn on the swing that he is currently using. Chris ignores her request and keeps the swing to himself. Irritated and miffed by his 'callousness,' the woman becomes increasingly insistent and loud in her demand. Finally, Chris tells her to wait until he is finished using the swing, after which, he says, the toddler will have

156

his turn. That, of course, does not sit well with offended Grandmother. She orders Chris to stop whatever action game he is involved with and let the toddler on the swing immediately.

Tension mounts quickly. Gretchen recognizes the danger of the situation for Chris. She signals time-out with her hands but to no avail. Chris is getting really agitated. She tries next to escort him in time-out, as she had done in the past with similar situations, but has to step back. Chris starts kicking and yelling. He is heading for the most explosive meltdown ever. Venting and raving, increasingly out of control, Chris starts to shout at the elderly lady, calls her names and starts throwing stones at her. Many people have gathered in shock and disbelief at what they see. They make comments: Why is the mother doing nothing to stop this? If that would be me, a good spanking to teach him better and the kid would be sent to bed tonight without dinner.

This has a galvanizing effect on Gretchen. She pulls herself right out of her own destructive emotions toward the whole situation and toward her child and starts to feel newly found compassion for what her son is going through. She becomes extremely calm. She sees the whole scene vividly and in slow motion, as if looking in from the outside. She is getting very clear on how to best help him. Chris is still pacing back and forth furiously. Pulling from her deepest resolve to hold her stand no matter what and not to feed any negativity at any cost by having a response that would not be a true consequence, she turns her back to the crowd and faces her son as if to offer a protective wall with her body. Very matter-of-factly, she calmly says to him in that neutral voice that signals time-out, "Right now, this is not a good place for you to be; let's leave." Mom says she could almost 'see' the battle going on in his head as he tries to calm down and apply some kind of internal brakes to stop the fury inside. Torn between two equally strong and conflicting emotions, he attempts some additional and menacing moves toward the lady only to retreat back to safety toward Mom. He obviously is still struggling to make up his mind whether or not to leave in time-out, as Mom says. He still needs to test her resolve at holding her ground and at not giving any payoff in terms of her energy for breaking the 'no fits of anger' rule, despite such tremendous pressure. He finally realizes that his antics are not going to work. All of a sudden, as if she has become the embodiment of time-out herself, he runs and throws himself into her arms, shaking and sobbing violently, until the intensity of the rage has left his body.

What consequence Chris got for breaking the 'no fits of anger' rule when they got home does not matter. But this was the last rage episode Mom and Chris would ever have to go through in their journey toward healing and transformation.

Michele, your beautiful synopsis of what happened here is a deep and lovely teaching. This is an amazing demonstration of the indomitable spirit of ruthless compassion and intent to support by a mother living and teaching a pivotal warrior lesson within this seeming parental nightmare.

Michele had expertly given this mother the tools and mental preparation for these critical moments of battle. The prize here is the alliance of a lifetime with a son who will never forget his mother's fortitude in those dark moments of forgetting his own. What a remarkable means to help this boy in battle mode learn and return to his place of peaceful power!

By not rewarding negativity at all costs, and removing the child to a place for a constructive consequence (without ongoing humiliation and negativity), Gretchen shined a light in this dark tunnel. Every parent faces at least one battle like this: the one that MUST be won, because the inner terrain of success is so worth fighting for. Bless this mother for knowing this was that critical battle! JLE

What an account of fortitude and determination. Expertly taught the principles of the Nurtured Heart Approach by Michelle, this mother had the bigger picture, the great wisdom, the great power and the presence of mind to discern what the moment called for.

The approach is not a prescribed set of strategies that are written in stone. In this approach, consequences are about conveying to the child the perception that there has been a result of his actions. The result is muddied when energy and relationship transpire in the midst of the negative experience. The magnitude of the child's experience of having a consequence is heightened by his experience of missing out, which is integrally related to how powerfully the parent has shifted relationship, energy and messages of success to the times when the problems are not happening. The exact way this is done will always differ in every family.

We don't know what the consequence was with this child, but it could have been as simple as Gretchen saying, as they walked away, "Thank you, Chris, for doing your time-out and getting it over with. You are handling so many strong feelings well right this moment. You could have continued raging but you didn't. You allowed yourself to feel your sadness and allowed yourself to be comforted."

The beauty of this approach is that the mother set the stage by not feeding Chris' negativity. Therefore, she could have simply created for Chris the illusion that he had a result of his actions by declaring the time-out over. And by so doing, she would have created a fresh 'now' in which she could further awaken his growing control, wisdom and power.

And apparently she did. Chris came to see that there was no longer any magic in acting-out, only in exercising his newfound greatness of choosing not to rage. This is the awakening: Chris awakening to his power and ability to be in charge in positive ways. And this could not have happened if his mom had chosen a fearful or angry response. He now has an internal template in development in which his private thoughts will begin defaulting to success rather than to negativity, anger, fear and doubt. He will attract relationships in life that will support the same, and he won't attract relationships that are based on problems. That's the inner side of the transformation that he will continue to develop and enjoy for the rest of his life. *HNG*

The Magic Is in the Positivity, Not the Consequences

By Dana Parkoff

I live in Dallas with my husband, Seth, and our five children. I have experienced my own family's transformation using the Nurtured Heart Approach, and it has been most natural for me to create a way to share it with other parents, educators and mental health professionals. I share this story as just one of the many examples of the incredible power of the Nurtured Heart Approach.

Our daughter, Sara, was 7½ years old and very challenging. She was regularly having outbursts, throwing tantrums, yelling, showing aggression, fighting and arguing with siblings. She would not do her homework, and she could never take "no" for an answer. Before we found help, she was screaming in my face. I felt maybe there was something wrong with her, and maybe there was something wrong with me as a mother. We had tried many published methods like 'Love and Logic' and '1-2-3 Magic' and others, even homeopathy and herbs. While all of the other parenting approaches worked pretty well with my other children, all backfired with her, often escalating the problem.

Feeling defeated, we finally took her to a therapist, but that didn't do much except give lots of energy to her problem. The one exception was that we did get a great recommendation for a neuropsychologist to do some testing. At the end of the intake session, the neuropsychologist mentioned I might find *Transforming the Difficult Child* to be helpful. Wow, was she ever right! Within days after implementing the approach, we saw immediate changes! We cancelled all therapy and delayed the testing until six months later, at which time no ADHD or ADD was found. She has minor language processing issues and some anxiety (read INTENSITY!).

This story about my daughter is one of the many first-hand experiences I share when I teach my parenting classes. I tell struggling parents to trust the process and their inherent ability to be the "agent of change" for their child – to relentlessly use the approach and remember that the magic is in the 'positivity' not the consequences.

One day Sara showed me five lollipops that she said her teacher had given her in school as a reward. I thought it was a little odd. The teacher is a friend of mine, and I was curious to mention it to her, but neglected to do so and let it go. The next morning, I went in my closet. There was a step stool right under a shelf where I happened to keep a large bag of lollipops to give out on our Sabbath. The bag was left open. I wasn't sure what to do.

I first wanted to give my daughter the opportunity to tell me the truth. I went into her bedroom and told her that I thought her teacher was so generous to give her so many lollipops. I suggested that it would be nice for her to write a thank-you note and that I wanted to be there when she delivered it so I could see the happy expression on the teacher's face. My daughter screamed, "Noooooooooo! I am not writing a thank-you note!"

I told her that maybe we could just go together and she could say thank you in person. She again said "Nooooooo!" and said it wasn't THAT teacher anyway, it was a different teacher who gave them to her. I suggested that she thank THAT teacher. Still, she didn't go for it.

I was disappointed that she didn't take this as an opportunity to come clean. Although I was tempted to lecture her on the value of being honest and not lying, I stuck to my Nurtured Heart resolve. I remained calm and collected, and despite my disappointment, I did not leak negativity. On the way to school that morning, I passed her a note. It read:

> Dear Sara, I need you to take a time-out for lying to me about the lollipops. I know you took them from my closet. In addition, when you get home from school, I will need you to clean the kitchen set in the playroom as a community service. (I use the community service element of the approach as a way to get my child back into doing good deeds.)

I watched in the rearview mirror as she read the note. She looked up and stared straight at me. I told her to let me know when she was starting her time-out. She remained quiet and calm, so 10 or so seconds later I said, "Looks like you just took it. It's over. I appreciate you taking responsibility for your actions. It shows integrity." I dropped the kids off with an "I love you" and a hug.

That afternoon, when I picked her up from school, she got in the car with a smile. After some pleasant conversation, I mentioned that the toys she needed to clean would be the kitchen set and the plastic food. She said okay. I immediately praised her for her cooperation and good attitude!

By the time I got inside to our playroom, I could see her with a spray bottle of cleaner and some paper towels! I told her that doing her time-out and community service with such a good attitude shows honesty, integrity, accountability for her actions, and owning up to her mistakes. After that, I continued to point these particular traits out to her every chance I could.

About a week later she asked for a lollipop. I told her that since she was such an honest and trustworthy person, she could go into the cupboard to get it herself. Now she sees herself as honest and trustworthy! Now that's inner wealth!

I started sharing the approach with friends, and I attended the advanced training with Howard Glasser in January 2007. I am now happy to be an advanced trainer, teaching parenting classes, doing private coaching in person and via telephone, as well as training teachers and school administrators in the Nurtured Heart Approach.

I am an observant Jew and have found the Nurtured Heart Approach concepts to be totally consistent with Judaism. In fact, I teach a teleconference class to Jewish women on the approach. They LOVE it and the word has spread quickly. While I use the approach more intensely with my challenging child, I have found it to be a beautiful way to run my home.

In my family, and in most of the families I have worked with, there is the challenge of dealing with the child's initial or sporadic resistance. I know that even if my child has an emotional 'setback' so to speak, it does not mean the approach is not working.

Now I understand the power of and the ability to 'reset' myself whenever I realize I am leaking negativity. While effective consequences are consistent, the perfect consequences are not punitive or long-lasting.

The power of change is really about how one can always find the positive in any situation!

A teacher for more than 20 years, Dana teaches parenting classes and trains teachers and school administrators in the Nurtured Heart Approach. As a Certified Nurtured Heart Specialist, she also does private coaching in person and via telephone. Dana is a featured presenter at the Annual Dallas Conference for Jewish Women. Finding the Nurtured Heart Approach to be consistent with Judaism prompted Dana to develop a parenting class geared specifically for Jewish women. This seven-week teleconference class has enabled her to teach Jewish women all over the world!

I remember a family when I first started teaching this approach, years before it even had a name. They had a young daughter about 8 years old who had a host of ways of challenging her family. Her mom and dad rose to the occasion and were fairly fast in adapting to this alternative way of parenting that I recommended. They quickly came to be solid in all the components of the approach, and within a few weeks almost all the problem behaviors fell away. All except one, that is.

The one behavior that remained was minor incidents of stealing. But for both parents, stealing was not just any normal problem; it was major with a capital M. Had it been viewed as just one more way their daughter had become accustomed to getting intense relationship, I am positive that this would not have remained an issue.

However, since the daughter detected that this had so much juice and remained so alive for her parents, she remained stuck in her addiction to the tremendous intimacy she perceived to be available through these acts of stealing.

The problem was that, although the parents were making great strides in every other way, everyone remained stuck as a result of this one issue. The 'transformation' could not happen until their daughter could experience a new truth – that her parents could get out of the way and let her break this rule like any other rule without falling into the trap of delivering the truckload of energetic 100-dollar bills in exchange for the adversity.

Luckily they eventually got it and started treating this rule like any other and began to make the excited responses whenever the 'no stealing' rule was not being broken. The transformation happened when the daughter realized there was no longer any allure and magic left for breaking any rules, including the rule about stealing. All the magic was for making great choices.

When I read Dana's story, I was holding my breath waiting to see how it would be handled. I couldn't be more thrilled when the story unfolded in this perfect way. Dana gave no indication that stealing was treated with greater relationship. Dana reset herself beautifully when she sensed she indeed held a potentially greater charge there. It was also so wise that she created a scenario where her daughter was accused of the success of handling her time-out beautifully and that she followed the scene with powerful compliments. Dana is so right that keeping the time-out short and sweet set the stage to show that there was no major 'juice' for this one rule over others. It totally allowed for this sweet outcome.

I love that Dana is taking the Nurtured Heart Approach to the Jewish community and that she finds it aligned to Jewish Scriptures. Many others among our advanced trainers have found an alignment to other sacred texts and are bringing it to the realms of Christianity, Catholicism, Buddhism and so on. A Native American elder once told me after a presentation that the Nurtured Heart Approach is beautifully aligned with the Hopi Way. Ultimately I hope that this approach turns out to be aligned with the core beliefs of every way. **HNG**

I smile every time I read Dana's heart-warming story because I know it's going to have a happy ending. Dana's relentless vision and action to hold and create only 'positivity' virtually guarantee a success-built outcome. It is one thing to look for the good stuff, but it's another to be so steeped in faith beyond the setbacks that you literally are creating a positive outcome together with your child.

Dana shares with us the essence of how not to fall in the cracks of fear or negativity, as well as her wonderful version of consequences. She offers perfectly timed acknowledgments to seal the deal for a seamless consequence that works and leaves her daughter with fortified integrity and a clear motivation to *do the right thing in the future! Consequences that engender integrity, truthfulness and family values are Dana's message. Fear, shame or anger may result in compliance for some, but Dana chronologies how love, patience and faith walk the highest road to instill and support core values.*

I love the trust and the recognitions Dana offers her daughter as she asks appropriately for a lollipop later. It is proof that our children rise to the level of trust and greatness we expect, and the deepest, most profound teachings can be offered without punishment, lectures or heavy hands. Sometimes the perfect consequences are not the weight of the consequences, but the 'positivity' that frames them. Thank you, Dana, and bravo to your wise Lollipop Girl for showing her integrity in her own creative way! JLE

Limits Like their Lives Depended Upon It

By Jamie Harr and Dawn Duncan-Lewis

Children who have known no healthy limits look for them like their lives depended on it. Like a person who is drowning, they can be trying to get their needs met in violent, unproductive ways; it can be almost impossible to give them what they need.

Bobby was a 10-year-old boy when he came to his new school, a school for K-12 children who have been identified as having emotional and behavioral disorders. At Bobby's intake session with school personnel, he was accompanied by his grandmother (who was, at that time, his primary caregiver), his case manager and his counselor. Bobby's soon-to-be new teacher, Mrs. H, could tell right away that Bobby would be a good candidate for her classroom.

Bobby could not sit still for the intake, and when the principal placed his binder on the table, Bobby kept tapping and pushing on it. He also interrupted the adults with such fervor, asking questions and making demands, that he was making it very difficult to carry on with the meeting. Even though Mrs. H needed to be present for the intake, she realized that Bobby had limits to his ability to participate in the meeting. Mrs. H volunteered to take Bobby for a walk in order to give the others a chance to talk, which would also give her a chance to get to know Bobby personally. During their walk, Mrs. H could tell that Bobby's attention span was very short, but she could also see a side to him that seemed sweet and polite. He had won her heart.

Meanwhile, with Bobby out of the room, Bobby's grandmother and counselors told the school staff that they were, at that time, looking for a residential mental health placement for Bobby. His grandmother appeared to have reached her limit with him. She doubted whether she would be able to keep herself, his brother and Bobby safe due to Bobby's constant violent behavior, aggressive arguing, and all-out challenges to her authority.

They also gave us a brief outline of what Bobby's life had been like until he and his brother had come to live with their grandmother. The boys, it turned out, had experienced many moves, their mom's regular use of drugs and alcohol, had been physically abused, witnessed domestic violence, and had a number of people in and out of their lives.

Our school therapist suggested a developmental assessment on Bobby. She explained that children who have lived highly stressed and chaotic lives often have developmental delays socially and emotionally, even though their 'thinker' may be closer to their chronological age. The assessment showed that this boy was at a stage of 2½ to 5 years old socially and behaviorally (which could, at least in part, explain his impulsivity and tantrum behaviors). Inside this 10-year-old was a frantic toddler trying to get his needs for structure and nurturing met. Cognitively, Bobby showed to be closer to his chronological age, which could be what made him such a REALLY good arguer.

We gave Grandma and the counseling staff a copy of the Nurtured Heart Approach book and briefly explained the program, including how the skills it teaches adults are exactly the nutritional elements that children need to help them with their social and emotional development. The counselors and Grandma said they would work together to read the book and learn the skills the book offered, and the meeting was over. We were ready to go.

As Bobby began school with Mrs. H and her Instructional Assistants, what we had learned from Bobby's assessment became evident from a practical standpoint. It was indeed going to be challenging to Bobby's teachers to teach a student who was functioning emotionally at age 2½ to 5, but academically was right on or above grade level. Mrs. H knew right away what her job needed to be: set clear limits and keep this boy busy, much as you would do with a two- or three-year-old. She also had to make sure Bobby had school work at his level and something to keep his mind occupied all the time. When she and her staff could keep him engaged in his work, life was good for everyone.

Bobby loved to sit by Mrs. H and, if things were going fine, that's where Bobby sat. When Bobby participated in his class' spelling contest, he always won, but his teachers found that he needed a lot of reassurance because it was really hard for him to win. Bobby, as with most of our students, did not take compliments very well, so staff had to be very careful when they gave him Kodak Moments (Active

167

Recognitions). Noticing students out loud came easily for Mrs. H though, and she found that her ability to be honest and to reflect back to Bobby what she 'saw' in him helped her build a trusting relationship with him. As Bobby began to trust his teacher and accept her honest feedback and positive noticing of his successes, he also became able to accept Mrs. H's corrections and 'resets' or time-outs.

Working with Bobby at school was often like riding a bucking bronco – he was so excited and full of energy, but determined to use whatever ways he had at his disposal to try to get his needs for attention and nurturing met. His mind seemed to be racing a hundred miles an hour. He needed to know what was going on and why. He argued every point presented if he didn't understand or agree. Mrs. H knew that she could not feed the negativity he was SO good at producing and that he also needed VERY consistent structure.

There were five rules in Mrs. H's class, which the students had helped create. One rule was "no swearing" and anyone who swore would automatically owe Mrs. H a one-minute time-out. That was the rule and the consequence, no matter what. Bobby tried to get around the rule by spelling "H-E double hockey sticks" but Mrs. H didn't let him down. Without looking at him and with as little emotion in her voice as possible, she said, "Take a time-out." And he did. Mrs. H's motto for broken rules was, "Take the consequence and come back ready to get back to work."

Bobby knew that the rule and the consequence were consistent and that no one was going to continue talking with him afterward about the mistake he had just made. Mrs. H knew that this consistency not only helped Bobby's social skills around not swearing, but also gave him the feeling of security he needed to progress in his development. Mrs. H's welcoming response when Bobby, or any student, returned from a time-out ("Bobby, I'm so glad you're not missing this because I know you like...") also helped him feel special, like the class really needed his input, and they did.

One of the biggest challenges to school staff as a whole was when Bobby would really fly off the handle, which he could do at any time and without warning. Bobby would become very animated, swear, yell, and kick or bite anyone who happened to be nearby. He would say things like "I hate you!!" or "It's not fair!" to anyone within ear shot.

Mrs. H worked very patiently with the rest of the school staff to not give Bobby any attention when he was in one of these states, but he could be VERY compelling. Eventually, though, the rest of the staff got onboard and before long, we were noticing that Bobby was taking less and less time to get himself calmed and back to work. Mrs. H believed he could do it and he did!

Grandma and Bobby's counselors reported that they were all using the Nurtured Heart skills with Bobby, including noticing him out loud, enforcing Grandma's rules and not giving attention to Bobby's negative behaviors. They, too, were noticing a dramatic change in Bobby. He was generally calmer, able to sit with Grandma to talk or while she read to him and his brother, and generally more relational. He was arguing with his Grandma less and using his words more calmly when he wanted to discuss something. AND, he had quit fighting with his brother! Physical fights were one of Grandma's greatest concerns at the intake, and the fighting had stopped!

It had been only four months since Bobby's intake and things seemed to be going pretty well. Bobby had become very responsive to Mrs. H and her staff's tutelage, his behavior had made marked improvement, and he was becoming a responsible, successful student. So when Mrs. H heard from Bobby's counselors that they and Grandma wanted to set up a new appointment to talk about his placement again, we were very surprised!

It turned out that Grandma was again feeling that she was loosing ground with Bobby and was feeling overwhelmed. Our school therapist said, "Let's do another assessment and see what's going on." We found that Bobby had matured behaviorally and socially one whole stage of development IN FOUR MONTHS!

So what was happening that he should now have become such a problem for Grandma again? It turns out that, instead of being a very intense toddler, he was now a very intense early elementary-age person, a stage much closer to his chronological age! With that came all of the challenges adults can face with children in that stage, with Bobby's own style of challenges and personality thrown into the mix. It seemed like, for this child, normal developmental challenges were there, but for him the volume was turned up to almost unbearable decibels!

We told Grandma, "Congratulations! You've been a success at helping your grandson mature to his next set of challenges!" She smiled. We encouraged Grandma to go home and not to let up on the Nurtured Heart strategies she had learned. In fact, we advised her to crank her Nurtured Heart skills up to match Bobby's developmental volume!

We were also noticing behavior changes in Bobby at school. Bobby's new developmental stage is characterized by needing to look good to and be noticed by others. For Bobby at first, this meant that he could no longer stand his peers looking at him in class; at the same time, he began to cause trouble for them by flipping them off or mouthing inappropriate words to them. We maintained our Nurtured Heart structure, tried hard to not miss a chance to give Bobby appreciation and recognition, and continued to refuse to give energy to his negative pleas for attention.

Eventually, Bobby was able to begin to interact with his peers in more positive ways. It happened in small moments, a little at a time at first; we tried not to miss an opportunity to notice his emerging skills out loud. Watching Bobby grow was like watching a time-lapse photo of a rose unfolding. His negative behaviors were so visible and loud that every increment of improvement was also very noticeable.

Soon, we were able to celebrate with him that he was indeed becoming a social person. It was interesting to note though that, as Bobby interacted increasingly with peers, he seemed to hold them to the same level of accountability to which he held himself and the adults in his life, too. We began to think we may have a future leader here. It wasn't as easy for his peers to accept this tendency as a future gift to the world, however. Oh, well, it seems there is always room for growth.

By the end of that school year, Bobby's home school district was lobbying for his return to his home school. Bobby's grandmother had managed to restore relative calm to her home and family again. She was somewhat nervous about Bobby returning to a general education setting so soon. She did decide, however, to give it a try.

It had been a wild ride for us all, and it seemed to end somewhat abruptly, but we were happy for Bobby's and his grandmother's successes. Bobby was growing up nurtured toward success and a more positive potential; we imagine he will do great things some day!

Jamie and Dawn offer us an amazing chronology of 'bronco boy' Bobby's miraculous unfolding into his greatness, because in part these wonderfully committed healers saw beyond the terrible terrain and held a strength-focused vision for Bobby and his grandmother – with strong limits and recognitions as the foundation. This definitely was not a cakewalk transformation here. It was HARD WORK! Setting limits relentlessly "like their lives depended upon it" really is the winning mantra here – and Bobby's life did depend on it.

This story describes the deep healing that is possible, even given a child's horrific history that might have jaded even the best teachers and counselors. It seems the essential healing task was really about finding the right combination of emotional nutrition and strong, predictable limits/consequences to help Bobby's rather broken spirit mend and fly again.

The creative and relentless support of Bobby's high energy and bright mind for constructive endeavors was another key here. Jamie and Dawn were diligent in providing a continual stream of recognitions and essential coaching for grandmother. She, too, blossomed with a new perspective and success toolbox to perceive and support her dynamo grandson and his greatness. Congratulations, grandmother, for seeing YOUR greatness and capabilities in the process as well! A deep bow to a dynamic duo, Dawn and Jamie, for working a full-spectrum, multi-generational family healing through diligence and eyes on the high road! JLE

A deep bow from me as well to Jamie and Dawn, to the school team and to Bobby and his grandmother. Combined, their efforts not only pulled this boy into his new world of experiencing and being his greatness – who he really is – but their efforts perhaps will change generations to come. How many others will Bobby's new light impact, how much will grandmother have to share with others now that she has experienced to the core how her concerted efforts have transformed this child, and how much more confidently will Dawn, Jamie and their entire team march on to help *so many others? Virtually no child is a lost cause, and an approach can indeed make a world of difference. I hope all involved can hear me applauding all the way from Tucson, Arizona.* **HNG**

Jacob's Story

By Erin Whitney

I am a Licensed Professional Counselor in Texas and work with behavior-disordered children and teens. My own son Jacob, our oldest (and now 8), was always a super high-energy child who literally ran rings around us as parents and around anyone in his path! By the time he was 4, I had become one of those parents who dreaded going to pick him up from daycare – not because I did not want to see him, but because I knew that I would be greeted at the door with a laundry list of his misbehaviors that day. Often he was in the Director's office when I came to pick him up. Here I was, having the same sort of problems with my own son as I was hearing from the parents of the children I worked with at the counseling office! I was beginning to feel like a failure both as a mother and a counselor. After all, if I couldn't keep my own son 'under control,' how could I possibly help others?

I had tried everything I knew (which, as a counselor, was considerable) to help my son make good behavioral choices, to no avail. The final straw came when I took my first business trip since having Jacob, who was then 4. I had barely started the trip when I received a phone call from my husband saying, "Honey, we need to talk about YOUR son." I knew it couldn't be good! Jacob had been suspended from his pre-school that day for stabbing another child with a fork! We dealt with it as best we could, saying (once again) that we needed to "crack down" on his behavior. We were using the renowned '1-2-3-Magic' program at the time; it had worked for approximately three days before it backfired in a huge way.

When we tried to give Jacob time-outs using this program, he would kick the walls or cabinets so hard that I thought he was going to break his foot or the wall or both. If we put him in his room, he would literally "trash" the room, pulling down drapes, knocking over and emptying the dresser drawers, and pulling everything out of the closets. It was a disaster! One of my out-of-town friends came to visit during this time and was horrified at what happened when we gave him time-out.

We took him to a counselor who diagnosed him with ADHD and Oppositional Defiant Disorder (meaning that he wouldn't do ANYTHING that any adult wanted him to do without a HUGE fuss, if he would do it at all). He was also diagnosed with childhood depression and was referred to a psychiatrist for medication for all his symptoms. I was very opposed to medicating him, but I was about to give in because I did not know what else to do. And my husband aptly pointed out that we had to do something!

Fortunately, a flyer for Howard Glasser's workshop on 'Transforming the Difficult Child' came across my desk at work and I signed up. I attended the seminar with a huge chip of skepticism (because I had tried lots of methods already, with no relief in sight) and a tiny glimmer of hope (because a mom never gives up!). By the end of the seminar, even though some of the methods seemed 'upside-down,' I had decided to try the approach EXACTLY as Howard Glasser prescribed, because one thing was sure: what I was doing was NOT working!

I went home and started using the method that night. Within three hours (yes, hours) of Recognitions and Appreciations, my son's behavior began to change dramatically. I was careful to use a strong intensity of intervention with my son because his behaviors were incredibly intense.

On the third day, in the process of introducing time-outs, I said to Jacob, "Now, I'm going to be watching to see what you do, how well you take your time-outs. A good time-out means you take it quietly and right away, and then you get out!" That day, Jacob was in time-out more than not, but I knew my job was to tell him when he needed a time-out and to recognize any small step in the right direction. The very first time he even LOOKED toward the time-out spot when I said a time-out was needed, I made an immediate Recognition: "Good! You looked at it; that's where you need to go, right!" That was it. Then, the first time Jacob made just one step toward the time-out area when I told him to go, I said, "Great, you took one step toward time-out – you really know where you are supposed to go!" Then I did the same thing for three steps and then five steps toward the time-out area. Later that day, Jacob finally went all the way to the chair. I was all over that with strong acknowledgments, and as soon as he got there, he was done with the time-out. We were both thrilled and shared the moment of success together! Within one week, Jacob gradually got it! He went to time-out every time.

Whenever he was not in a time-out, I gave him many Kodak Moments and Recognitions. At one point, he had his hands over his ears, yelling "No Mommy, stop it! I don't like it!" I just kept recognizing his efforts, responding to his upset feelings with comments like, "I see you have these big emotions. It's good that you are able to tell me how you are feeling."

I did not let up on the method throughout his complaining and screaming that he didn't want me to continue appreciating him. All of a sudden a few days later, it was as if there was a click of the switch and the light bulb went on inside Jacob. I could almost hear him saying to himself, "I can tell you how I feel and don't have to get in trouble by acting out!" In that moment, Jacob burst out in tears with these words: "I'm so sad you never get time with me. The baby gets all your time!" Now he tells me how he feels more often and his behavior is better, too.

Soon after that big day of time-outs, we were in a restaurant having breakfast. Jacob was actually sitting (amazing, considering his strong hyperactivity), eating and carrying on a great conversation with me. I was using the approach with him, stating how I was enjoying sitting and eating and talking with him. Then he did a new thing with his fork. Instead of stabbing someone with it, he put it down, looked me in the eye and said, "And Mommy, you're not so mad at me anymore." Within three days, the Nurtured Heart Approach had not only transformed my son's behavior, it had begun to heal our strained relationship as well. Tears poured out of my eyes and I said a silent prayer that this method would continue to work. It has.

About a year after I started using the Nurtured Heart Approach at home, the out-of-town friend who had visited previously came to visit again. When she heard me give Jacob a time-out, she cringed and gave me a petrified look. She then sat with her mouth agape as Jacob calmly went to his time-out spot, counted his time-out himself and politely asked if he could go. This friend is a teacher who promptly enrolled in my Nurtured Heart class; she has virtually eliminated behavior problems in her classrooms. (In fact, she and her fiancée took the class together so that they can use it with any children they might have!)

In the four years since I first learned the approach, I have taught it to dozens of families, most of whom (approximately 85% of my clients) have had great success with it – with children and teens and also in a number of adult cases.

And Jacob? We have since moved and had to enroll him in public school instead of a private school. I worried about how he might do. On his first day, he brought home a 'Student of the Day' card, the first of many. We did not bother to tell this school about his diagnoses, and they have never mentioned any major problems or a desire to have him tested. In fact, during his second semester at the school, I went again to Arizona to attend Howard Glasser's week-long Advanced Training. While there, I received a phone call from my husband who said, "Honey, we need to talk about OUR son." (I admit, my heart went to my throat for a second.) Jacob had received 'Student of the Day' again and was doing a fabulous job of behaving well that entire week! In fact, he also received a difficult-to-receive commendation from school for exceptional conduct during one of the six-week sessions that year. P.S.: My husband finally learned the approach last year.

Jacob has simply excelled in every way possible since Nurtured Heart came into our home. He is happy most days and shows defiance only when under high stress. When this happens, I increase his 'dose' of Nurtured Heart techniques and his behavior goes back to normal. He is near the top of his gifted and talented class, he does well in Karate and he uses his intensity to create in fabulous ways! When we have dinner guests now, instead of disrupting the evening, he spontaneously makes placemats for everyone (accurately capturing their personalities!)

What would have happened to my son if I had not heard of this approach? I hesitate to even think of it. Instead, I'll continue to use the approach and to tell everyone I can about this wonderful miracle in our lives.

Erin Whitney provides personal coaching and seminars on the Nurtured Heart Approach to parents, educators and clinicians everywhere.

Erin could have succumbed to medication as management, as so many in such a struggle understandably do. The magic in this story's happy ending comes through her unshakable ability to meet Jacob's ultra high level of resistance and defiance with an equally high level of her own relentless force – a lens recognizing only success steps while ignoring the negatives. Her powerfully intentional structure literally shaped and formed baby steps of success for Jacob. By fearlessly following any literal step in the right direction (in this case, when Jacob even looked at or took two steps to the time-out chair), Erin succeeded in creating a compelling blend of emotional attention and nutrition for success steps. Lowering the rope just enough that Jacob was literally tricked into jumping over it becomes the momentum for him to run a new race toward compliance and, most importantly, his own personal sense of success and feeling appreciated.

Blessings to Jacob and Erin as they move beyond the struggle turf into the joyful, heartfelt territory of love and appreciation.
JLE

I was once in a room full of people where I witnessed Erin emotionally telling the story of Jacob and the fork. However, I never knew the rest of the story.

I love that Jacob confirmed for Erin with such certainty that he was aware all along about how mad she was and that he could now appreciate the difference. I love that Erin captured her great intensity in choosing to launch the approach intensively that very first day. I love that she was so creative in making that first time-out a reality. And I love that Erin was relentless and opportunistic in confronting Jacob every which way with notification of his successes. She accomplished all this despite having failures with many parenting methods and all the reason in the world to remain resentful of her child and dismissive of 'upside down' ideas that shake the reality of all she had diligently studied.

Most of all, I love that Erin gets to relish the new Jacob and his new victorious path of greatness — and the impact she has had on this wonderful child.

I am honored to know that Erin now shares her successes with the world and can influence so many other lives, including her teacher friend and the fortunate clients who find their way to her practice. *HNG*

Five Days to Transformation in a Kindergarten Classroom

**By Sherri Shober and
Katherine Walker Hutchinson**

I, Sherri Shober, have been a Kindergarten teacher in the same district for 10 years. The socio-economic status and cultural and ethnic diversity of our students had been changing. Our free and reduced lunch numbers were rising, as was the number of English language learners. Our minority population had broadened to include students who were African-American, Hispanic, Hmong, Pacific Rim, and immigrants from Liberia and Ghana.

This particular year, I found myself struggling with a class that did not have many pre-Kindergarten skills. The classroom was very loud and chaotic and the children were unable to follow a one-step direction. There was a lot of tattling, pushing, shoving and difficulty taking turns and managing personal belongings. There was little respect for people or property. The children were not responding to the usual techniques of teaching. Sadly, it wasn't a joy for me to come to school, and I questioned whether I wanted to teach anymore.

Katherine Walker Hutchison is a School-Family Liaison/Parent Educator who works in my Kindergarten classroom daily. Her job includes working with all students and their families to provide resources for academic achievement and tools for student success. It would turn out that we would become the transformation team for our young students.

Katherine had written and received a grant to fund six field trips for the year. We felt the 'Kinders' needed more experiences outside the classroom to improve vocabulary, build background and develop shared experiences. The planned trips included the zoo, the theatre, the nature center, the library and the grocery store. The first field trip was to an apple farm. Unfortunately, it was not a success. We had parents with us, but they were in the same condition as the children. They didn't understand what the rules were, so they could not manage or guide the children. After the field trip, we decided these field trips were simply out of the question. We were very sad. (More about this later.)

Speaking the Truth of What Needed to Change

Bad behavior had become the focus of the classroom; it had become a management nightmare. The traditional Kindergarten skills of letter and number recognition, sound development, social interaction and caring were taking a back seat. The students were already behind and everyday were falling farther and farther behind. The parents understood, because they had experienced similar behaviors at home.

The hope I offered parents was our registration for the Nurtured Heart workshop. Katherine and I would go as a team to seek strategies and techniques to help our students. It was called 'Transforming the Difficult Child,' and we knew we belonged there.

Howie Glasser and his approach 'spoke' to us as early childhood educators. Within the first few hours of the training, we were onboard with the approach and knew this highly intensive strategy was what we needed for our students. Katherine and I returned to our school ready to transform our Kinders. Our plan was to work as a classroom team until we got results. With the blessing of the principal, the timeframe we set was five days because Howie told us we could transform our classroom in five days and we believed him.

Starting Over – Five Days to Total Transformation

We began with a message to our Kinders that no one was happy, no one was learning, no one was having any fun. We were going to change that starting today. We asked them if they agreed. The overwhelming response was "yes." We all knew the environment was unsettling. We asked if they were ready for a new start. Again, the response was "yes." We said, "Let's cheer for a new start," and they all cheered. I told them Katherine would be part of our classroom and the new start.

Old Rules Get Clearer

Howie taught us to clarify and revise our classroom rules. All the rules were to begin with the word 'NO.' This was new to us. We had traditionally used rules such as "keep your hands to yourself," "show respect to others" and "be kind." Our new list included no hitting, no yelling, no somersaults, no jumping over chairs, no digging in others backpacks, and no biting.

Recognizing Clarity and Responsibility – a New Start

We asked each child to give us a rule. Every time a child came up with a rule, we gave the child verbal praise, a cheer and a small piece of candy. We wrote the new rules on a large piece of paper that we later hung on our classroom wall. We said this was starting over – a fresh start. We said these rules would help us be successful Kinders who could be kind and caring to others, learn letters and numbers, listen to a story, tell a story, learn to use a scissors correctly, learn new games and songs. The Kinders cheered for the change.

After about 45 minute of rule-making, we announced: "You can break these rules." They cheered and thought that was the greatest thing, saying "Yea! We're going to break these rules!" Then, in the next breath, we added, "Yes, you can break the rules, but if you break the rules, there will be a consequence." The consequence would be a time-out.

Revamping Consequences – a New Time-out

The class went silent. We said we are having a new start so there would be new time-outs, not the kind they were used to. First of all, there would be no more 5-minute timer, so we put that away in the closet. We continued to explain that the new time-out would start when they were quiet and not goofing around in the time-out chair. We would let them know when the time-out was over. We also told them we were not going to be upset if they broke a rule. Our new words would be *'Oops, broke a rule. Go take a time-out. I will let you know when you can come back.'*

We had a practice session: "Let's pretend somebody broke a rule and Ms. Shober will say 'Oops, broke a rule' without even explaining what rule was broken." We had many eager volunteers willing to demonstrate the new time-out. During the practice, we verbalized all the things the child was doing right (going to the time-out chair, how well he was doing during the time-out, thanks for not talking or kicking anyone, etc.). We all cheered the 'good' time-outs. The time-outs during this practice time were very short, and they seemed to love that! The children were totally engaged as we demonstrated.

There were no power struggles over this new practice. Some time-outs lasted for less than 30 seconds. Our philosophy was TIME-IN was more exciting than time-out.

Many Forms of Recognition as Anchors

At the beginning of our transformational week, we gave out many rewards. We knew we needed to match their intensity with words and with tangible rewards, mostly items that had always been in our classroom, but we just supplemented them with new items for instant appeal to the Kinders.

To recognize the class doing good work, we used a block collection system, putting big blocks into a large jar. Anytime during our day when we wanted to stress something positive (cooperation, sharing, taking turns, kind words, careful cutting), we would say "Table one, thanks for careful cutting, let's put in 4 blocks" or "table three, thanks for working without talking, let's put in 5 blocks because it is so hard to work without talking to our friends." When it was full, we'd have a class party or extra activities of the class' choosing that were curriculum-based. This gave the class power.

We continued to use our school-wide program of giving 'character slips' to a child who demonstrated good behavior. Not only was this slip a tangible token (the child would take it to the office to be placed in the box for the weekly drawing for the character medal for the week), but it was also an intrinsic reward. In the past we had given out character slips sparingly, but now we gave many to reinforce the desired behaviors. The Kinders were making an effort to practice the behaviors that would get noticed and they could now match their actions to the qualities of success.

Putting the Talk in the Walk

We extended out new methods of limits and consequences beyond the classroom. We practiced the procedures for lining up and walking in the hallway, being very intentional about the behaviors we did not want to see: no touching the walls, no bumping the person in front of or behind you, no swinging your arms, no hitting others, no loud voices, no complaining about not leading the line. We explained, "This is your choice. You can break these rules and there will be a consequence."

Widening the Net and Weaving a Community of Support

We emphasized to the children that time-out and time-in could take place anywhere, not just inside the classroom. We visited the principal, office staff, nurse and specialists. They all applauded the students for doing a great job of walking in the hall quietly as well as for characteristics such as strength, cooperation, self-control and respect. We sought out as many adults as we could in the school so the children would be receiving positive messages from many people. One of our goals was to let them know that the whole school was on their side!

We energized them whenever the rules were not being broken, something that was a new way for us. The Kinders were receiving clearer instruction and were really responsive to the emotional nutrition. They became empowered and we all supported their newfound strengths.

No Threats – Just Instant, Neutral Consequences

There were no threats, just instant time-outs for rule breaks and praise and recognition for positive behavior. "Thanks, Melissa, for following the directions to sit at your desk," which would make them all want to do the good thing and receive praise. We knew then that change was taking place. They wanted to cooperate and participate with us. *They knew we were different and they wanted to do the right thing.*

The children were calmer, but the classroom was still intense. What was different was the direction of the energy and we learned to appreciate their intensity. We could all get excited about the simplest things. There were short time-outs, but we focused on the time-ins for the rest of the children, making the time-ins more intense and rewarding. *We knew we were 'getting them' – helping them negotiate their environment so they had more positive power.* They learned they could get more of their needs met in a school setting! Finally, we think they felt understood.

Tag Team Energizing Success

Children watch adults' action all the time, yet infrequently is there discussion about the behavior – naming the behavior and giving the reason the behavior is helpful and why it should continue. Children want and need information about how to manage the real world, and Katherine and I were a live example. We were intense in complimenting one another, pointing out the good things each of us was doing. We were teaching good behaviors and qualities through example. The Kinders saw us as capable people and the successes between us.

This approach also taught us to be more reflective of our own methods and decisions – a way of evaluating a good idea or not such a good idea. After a not-so-quiet trip to the water fountain, we said "Maybe the next time we go for a drink, we'll take half the kids so it's not such a long wait and we don't have to leave our work in the class-room as long." We had never experienced this before because we were constantly trying to manage students' behavior. Now we could be reflective about things that worked well, too. We could do it with each other and with the students. They could observe our problem-solving model. They soon started offering ideas of their own to make improve-ments. Our classroom became a powerful place.

Transformations in the First Three Hours

We were so amazed with the transformations we observed in just the first three hours. For example, preparing to go to the lunchroom had always been one of our most challenging transitions previously. On that first day, we created a strategy about giving 'tips' to others and used this as a way to improve the trek to the lunchroom. "This is what it looks like when you walk into the lunchroom, hold your tray, wait in line. This is what your voice and body should be doing." We would then ask them, "What are some tips you can give to make everyone successful as a community"? We always acknowledged a good tip with a positive, energized response.

We wanted them to experience what it meant to create a nice place to be – where we could care about each other. We talked about how it feels when someone holds the door for you or picks up your napkin if you drop it – it makes our hearts feel good. We didn't assume that they knew how to behave or think about others. This was a change in our operating style. We talked about how important it was to "thank the lunch lady who worked so hard to feed you" and then gave instruc-tions on how to say thanks to the lunch staff. Again, we encouraged them to feel the feelings associated with doing the right thing as well, saying: "It feels great when you are thankful, doesn't it?"

We knew we were on the right path when the children were able to give others praise for successes.

Transformation Stories from Our Classroom

A Culprit Reborn. One day, several bottles of bubble mixture were found dumped out on the sidewalk. We decided to postpone the already earned 'extra recess' until the culprit was found. We said we were not going to be angry, we just wanted people to be honest and believe in themselves enough to tell us who had done it. Later, a student fessed up and we just calmly said, "Thank you for telling us." Without naming the student, we announced that we would be able to have extra recess options again. We openly said "The person had a lot of strength to come forward to admit to this." We also did a cheer for this anonymous person's strength. We dealt with this potential negative by focusing on the positives.

Keeping the Positives Already Earned. Our rules about filling the block jar for earning group rewards were clear. Students could add a block only if directed to do so. The old rule was that if any unauthorized blocks were added, the whole jar was dumped out.

One day, a half-full jar magically became full. The class was very upset, concerned about the consequences for the whole class based on the misbehavior of one. They had all worked so hard with their positives to fill the jar. The option of starting over seemed overwhelming to them. So we strategized how to keep the positives already earned, rather than taking things away. We also asked for the children's input to solve our dilemma. In the end, the class decided they wanted to go ahead and have 'half a cookie and half a video party' that day rather than wait for the jar to refill.

So we proceeded with cutting the already small cookies in half, and the video was stopped right at the suspenseful halfway point, but no one cried or fussed. They really seemed to get it. They understood this was the plan they had agreed upon and it was fair for us to follow through as decided.

Deciding about a consequence for the student who filled the jar against the rules was also a good experience for the class. The student came forward on her own soon after we discovered the jar. She was very upset and sobbing over the incident. The class brainstormed several options for consequences. She could miss the whole party, she could miss half the party, she could apologize to the class, or she could attend the half cookie and video party that day after a brief time-out.

During the process, the students were quite calm and compassionate, recognizing it was hard but good to tell she had filled the jar; she was strong yet made a bad choice. The class decided to let her choose her consequence from the options presented. She chose to apologize to the class and attend the party after serving a brief time-out.

This incident ended with many positives. There were no overly punitive consequences (deprivation of all privileges) based on one person's negative behavior. The culprit learned from a quick time-out and a simple yet powerful act of community service (a group apology) within the context of a compassionate, forgiving classroom. Once again, it was a two-fold learning process for the class and for the young student.

Our Pledge to Keep the Lunchroom Clean. We decided to use the Nurtured Heart Approach to deal with children leaving messes in the lunchroom as well. First we defined the problem. We told the children it wasn't the custodian's job to clean up after them, he had bigger issues to deal with like the boiler and fire safety in the building. We emphasized we could take care of ourselves and were committed to having a clean lunchroom, both for ourselves and the second graders who use the lunchroom after us. We went over each appropriate cafeteria behavior. Next, we discussed how a pledge was a promise and it was important to stick to it. The children agreed to take a pledge to the custodian; we would do our part to make his job easier, and we were serious about taking care of ourselves and the cafeteria. Then we all met with Tony, our custodian, discussed his role and their pledge to him to engage in appropriate cafeteria behaviors and cleanup

Including the children in this powerful example of proclaiming their responsibilities and commitment would be tested the next day and the next. The transformation was beyond wonderful.

The first day, the entire class was not only under their own table picking up napkins and silverware from the floor, they were helping to clean under every cafeteria table – a virtual group cleaning patrol for anything on the cafeteria floor!

New Parent-Teacher Alliances

One of our strategies was to call home or send notes home when a child was making great strides in replacing bad behavior with good behavior. This was contrary to the typical practice of calling home to report only on problems.

During parent-teacher conferences held after implementation of this approach, the parents noted that their children were coming home happy. Discipline problems were greatly reduced. Alliances of hope and support were beginning to be built with the parents of intense children.

One of the more memorable conferences was with the father of a boy who had previously been a big discipline problem. The father actually broke down in tears of relief and gratitude when we both confirmed the boy was no longer a discipline problem and was quite likeable in many ways. We recounted to the downtrodden father the child's strengths of working with others, a sense of humor and happier mood. The father admitted that this was the first time his son had not been labeled a major discipline problem, stating, "No one has ever said anything good about my son's behavior."

Those Field Trips

As you may recall, we had put all field trips on hold after the unsuccessful trip to the apple orchard. Now, with such success in transforming the classroom, we decided we would try another field trip but first we wanted to train a team of parents in the Nurtured Heart Approach. They would become field trip volunteers. Trained volunteers are happy volunteers.

We formed a team of parents who were willing to participate in the training and willing to help with the remaining five field trips we had planned through the grant. Katherine trained the parents in one hour, complete with handouts of the techniques, the rules, the quick time-outs, and language to use to show appreciation of good behavior.

The results were marvelous. We witnessed parents guiding children successfully. One parent avoided a power struggle with a child over walking on a bench. Her words were: "There is no walking on benches, I need you to walk with the group." Surprisingly the student jumped down, joined the group, and the parent said "Thanks for working with our group. I appreciate your listening and acting so quickly, that makes it fun at the zoo." A big smile emanated from the student.

Casting the Support Net Home

After the success of our field trip volunteer training, we wanted to give all parents some tips and ideas about what we had learned from this approach to use at home. We sent a 'guide sheet' home to each parent and invited each to come to school to meet with us and then observe the classroom.

Katherine actually sat in the back of the classroom with parents as they observed, pointing out Kodak Moments, Recognitions, the specific elements of an effective time-out and so on. Without exception, the parents couldn't believe what they were seeing. They couldn't believe that everyone was on task and working so well. It was such a powerful experience because we were all on the same page!

We really felt we were providing a big service to our families to see the approach in action. Everyone wants their child to be successful. This was a way parents could really see the possibilities.

Final Words about What Teachers Need

Teachers dealing with a classroom of high intensity children may need the support of a colleague to help them strategize and begin a new approach. Teachers also need to be given a period of time to be free of academic achievement goals and permission to take the time to put an approach like this in place – in service of greater social, emotional and academic achievement in the long run.

In this week of energizing and transforming this classroom, we were both exhausted, but it was so worth it. It takes energy to change energy.

Katherine Walker Hutchinson currently is a high school Family Consumer Science teacher and continues to use Nurtured Heart with her high school students and their families.

Katherine's primary philosophy is to set high expectations for all students, articulate them often and provide clear steps and support for success. Always energize the moment.

Sherri Shober believes that the step-by-step structure of the Nurtured Heart Approach is its success. "It is a freeing experience for me as a teacher to say, I'm not in charge of all of their choices; I can now say what is expected of them in the classroom and make it a positive environment." Because children are in charge of themselves via their personal choices, Sherri is able to focus more on being a stable element to provide positive energy and predictable, neutral consequences with amazing results.

I am so thrilled to witness by way of this great story the brilliance and determination of Sherri and Katherine. I love that they proceeded in an all-out, get it done, warrior way. It's always incredible for me to experience the greatness of highly trained educators and therapists who are willing to suspend all previously acquired knowledge to move forward with a new approach that takes an entirely different angle. I applaud their willingness to launch in this way.

I want to underscore the fantastic creativity Sherri and Katherine applied in aligning with parents. This is such a pivotal element, and to accomplish it so quickly is breathtaking. Bringing parents into a collaborative appreciation of the approach not only propels and deepens the impact in real time, but it creates a common language that, in my experience, softens or dissolves any of the typical kinds of barriers one can experience in real-life situations. So many parents have had their own diminished or even painful experiences in classrooms and school buildings as students themselves, and the normal educational protocol of calling home when problems are occurring can further alienate a parent who already steps into a school gingerly. This new approach of calling to point out successes and using the successes to inform parents of an alternative way to reach their child is a brilliant way of bridging that gap. The way they fed their new approach into field trips was brilliant, as was their contribution to the father's first-ever good news about his child's school behavior. Also brilliant was their exquisite experiment with appreciating each other and processing out loud for the benefit of the children.

I feel so blessed to be even remotely associated with how this classroom transformation played out and with how this wound up nurturing the hearts of so many. HNG

Sherri and Katherine offer us the kind of masterful inspiration in education that comes from reassessing and restructuring as veteran educators with a beginner's mind. This beautiful story of a five-day classroom transformation is full of concrete examples of creative refortifying with new means of leadership and calling forth the spirit of team-building among these amazing students. In realizing they were just putting out fires with energy and attention on the wrong end of the spectrum, Sherri and Katherine literally turn the whole classroom into an inspiring and energetic magnet of learning vital social skills and core human values of respect and appreciation. Their Kinders literally learn and transform their world with kinder energy! Their strategies to involve the whole school in supporting the children's transformation and then to extended the successes to the families resulted in an explosion of teamwork, positive change, esteem-building and a whole classroom now hooked into positives! Brilliant is their success formula: using individual and group Recognitions, teaching delayed gratification, awarding 'character' slips, and moving extrinsic rewards into heartfelt intrinsic experiences the children actually experience and embody. Sherri and Katherine's formula is composed of practical and incremental success. They also offer a great balance of teaching with a positive, energized focus along with meaningful rather than punitive consequences. The deepest, most true and organic change comes from the children's needs being met, seen and supported at their most fundamental level.

Offering classroom observation and coaching for parents to see and understand the approach in action, with guidelines to use at home, was brilliant community and family support!

Thank you, Sherri and Katherine, for a stunning, five-day prescription for transformation and success. May your Kinders go forth into the world grounded in their greatness, and may you both have the gift of seeing them shine in the future! JLE

The Master of "I Can"

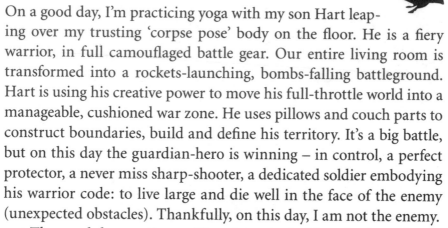

By Jennifer Easley

On a good day, I'm practicing yoga with my son Hart leaping over my trusting 'corpse pose' body on the floor. He is a fiery warrior, in full camouflaged battle gear. Our entire living room is transformed into a rockets-launching, bombs-falling battleground. Hart is using his creative power to move his full-throttle world into a manageable, cushioned war zone. He uses pillows and couch parts to construct boundaries, build and define his territory. It's a big battle, but on this day the guardian-hero is winning – in control, a perfect protector, a never miss sharp-shooter, a dedicated soldier embodying his warrior code: to live large and die well in the face of the enemy (unexpected obstacles). Thankfully, on this day, I am not the enemy.

The good day continues: Hart (content in his epic victory) uses his amazing imagination and visual artistry upon the drawn page. He spends an hour sketching his 'battle' comic strip, and redesigns his compound with blocks. The quieted warrior smoothly transitions through homework, dinner and the bedtime routine. Today is a 'good' day. It's a day when Hart is the master of "I can" all day long.

On a hard day, 'Sergeant Kai' (his military persona) re-enters the home compound, barking orders like a frustrated drill sergeant. He carelessly tosses his battle gear and uniform (backpack and coat) on the floor. His grenade (water bottle) impacts an adjoining wall, and a combat dagger (math pencil) takes a sacrificial dive into the top of our dining room table during the big battle (homework). If I issue a mandate (like "time to wash hands for dinner"), I'm being unreasonable. If a privilege is unavailable or removed as consequence, I am "horrible, the worst mother in the world," and according to the angry sergeant, someone he will "never trust again." He howls and growls crouched on the floor – a high drama, a Greek tragedy. I wonder whether I should issue the 'big order/edict,' retreat to the bathroom bunker or hunker down in my kitchen foxhole.

It is big work, this warrior stuff. I didn't realize what I signed up for – birthing this fire-warrior boy when I was age 41. My self-focused, child-free, peaceful, yoga world was brought to full attention through the warrior lessons learned mothering my most powerful, strong-willed son. It took three long and tiring years to realize that I was the biggest problem in Hart's behavioral maelstrom.

I remember well a traumatic episode holding Hart for 35 minutes after he charged me, fists and feet flying, like an angry kangaroo. We were covered with sweat and tears, exhausted, collapsing on the floor, when the sergeant finally surrendered. It was a mother's nightmare. Yet something inside told me I must win that battle to let Hart know he was safe and contained. Somehow, I needed to prove to Hart that I loved him too much to give up on his ability to learn self-control. I needed to show him I could meet and contain his energy in the absence of his 3-year-old ability to contain himself.

After several anguishing, exhausting episodes of 'loosing my cool,' yelling and handling the situation poorly, I became convinced that I was the problem instead of the solution. Admittedly, I was tired, depressed and too ashamed to ask for help. After all, shouldn't a Child Mental Health Specialist with over 15 years of experience with difficult children KNOW how to handle her OWN difficult child?

Hart was three when Howard Glasser, a dear friend and colleague, visited our home in Seattle while offering a seminar on his Nurtured Heart Approach. How perfectly synchronistic this was for me, the struggling mother. The divine and painful irony: I was the co-author of Glasser's book on the subject and coordinator for this local event. Nothing like a painful paradox to launch one tired mama into a new healing leap via her high-octave son and family therapy mentor!

It's embarrassing to be a Child Mental Health Specialist with an out-of-control child. Even worse, Hart was not responding at all to my gentle limits and nurturing – what I call 'soft parenting' (which works with many children). I was surprised to find myself both resisting using the Nurtured Heart Approach (which I knew well and had taught many families) and needing it at the same time. Clearly, I was the strong-willed, high-intensity mother requiring assistance herself. My ego did not surrender easily. It took Howie being in our home, watching me give Hart a half-hearted time-out, to bring me back to the right intention: to really commit to trusting and allowing my child to have a consequence in the face of breaking rules.

Hart was displaying the common misbehaviors of an oppositional 3-year-old, testing the limits and security of predictable parental responses. On this day, he yelled and hit me, so time-outs were warranted. "No hitting, Hart," I said in a firm, clear voice. "Go to time-out" (clear, and definite). A good start, no doubt. However, being a strong-willed child, testing for the upper hand, Hart started moving to our designated time-out chair, but kept blasting me verbally, rather than sitting down and becoming quiet (our clear time-out rules). Here is some of the verbal exchange between us and how I allowed my masterful warrior (then a toddler) to turn the tables of power by not offering him a true, meaningful consequence:

Hart: *You're an awful mommy! I hate you!* (verbal assault/smoke screen tactics; attempting to hold my attention through defiance)

Me: (ignoring the words that bore deeply into my heart) *Your time-out starts when you are in your chair and quiet.* (repetitive, predictable command offering energy and attention to Hart's opposition)

Hart: *I'm NOT going to take a time-out.* (holding firm in his battle objective negativity)

Me: *Come on Hart, just sit down, it's easy to do.* (I release my authority through issuing a lesser consequence and trying to soften it.)

Hart: *NO! I WON'T!* (Hart holding dramatically true to the upper hand position of power, gained and increasing.)

Me: *You will (pause) if you want to come and play again.* (Another reminder, weakening my position, with an attached threat to further challenge the soldier burrowing in for the battle.)

Hart: *I don't care!* (His clear declaration: threatening is an ineffective tool. Just another great hook Hart cleverly uses to bait me, because I do care.)

Me: *Your time-out starts when you are in your chair and quiet!* (I took the bait, hook, line and sinker with yet ANOTHER reminder.)

Hart: *I'm NOT going!* (Hart, firmly in control, tightens his hold on the fishing rod (power) with me as the easy 'catch of the day.')

Me: *You can do it, sweetie. Come on.* (Showing my cheerleader vulnerability, offering encouragement for opposition, clouding and cushioning the consequence.)

Finally, in that consequence-going-down-the-drain moment, Howie (thankfully) interceded with one powerful sentence – flowing from his eagle-like perception. With this one masterful sentence of Glasser greatness, I received the parenting lesson of my life: "Jenn, why don't you get out of the way and let Hart have a consequence?!"

There it was. Howard Glasser's fine, one-line tune-up for the whole cream-puff mother machine. A simple solution: Get out of the way and let your child have a consequence.

In my overprotective desire to spare my child (and perhaps myself) a long or difficult consequence, I was disallowing the opportunity of one at all, as well as setting the stage for many more. I was offering Hart a delicious portion of energy and attention for his negativity. It was unwittingly placed on the largest possible plate of continued conversation and persuasion, complete with a side-dish of walking on eggshells (as I cajoled him). Rather than unplugging from the negativity and conflict, my continued attention was fueling the fires of opposition and non-compliance – exactly the opposite of my objective.

Sometimes it takes a surrendered, exhausted state in order for the beauty and power of the beginner's mind, or what we already know yet resist, to take effect. This is often the territory parents with challenging children find themselves in, and it certainly was the case for me. Being in uncharted, uncomfortable territory, when the known or conventional does not work, is often when the magic change becomes most possible. (Ironically, a family counselor we were seeing after this incident with Howie happened to recommend the Nurtured Heart Approach for us. My husband and I enjoyed a laugh over this perfect paradox.)

Five years have passed since that fate-turning lesson of truth and healing offered by Howie and Hart in my surrendered moment of truth. I've realized mothering a strong-willed, intense and sensitive child is a warrior practice for me, too. With our willful leader-to-be, I need to hone my sword of parenting truth, of practicing heart-based support, and of being firm and clear with a consistent, clean response. I have learned the critical importance of offering Hart a true consequence rather than a softened, fuzzy one.

Well before that 'Howie moment of wisdom and exhortation,' I was conscious that my emotional response to Hart and his behavior would be my biggest challenge. From my first maternal angst when he was an inconsolable infant, the hook (my nervousness) was there. I was firmly attached to the misguided notions that I could always make it better; could take away his pain; or teach him to avoid the pain. Unfortunately, I can't.

Experienced parents of more than one child know this lesson best. Not only can we NOT take away a good deal of our children's angst, discomfort or pain, many children learn best through the uncomfortable road of struggle and consequences. For many children, good-sense lectures on caution, preparedness or good values do not translate as learning during a struggle phase. If we stand in the way of them learning through experience (including consequences), we are both part of the problem and a reason the learning process and struggle are prolonged.

Learning the 'hooks' and how to internally dismantle/unweave my core issues around them was the biggest work and greatest labor of love for me. For example, one major hook was Hart's crying and wailing for me to do something, give him something – a desired toy, instant food, or help him complete a task he was struggling with. That plea of "Mom, I can't do it! Help me!" goes right into the primitive mama brain, somehow internally translating as a life-and-death response system. Now, I recognize these pleas as signs of Hart's need for more Acknowledgments and Recognitions of any act in the direction of mastery – independence, task persistence in the face of frustration, patience or not giving up. I, too, am forced to manage my own intensity: to maintain calm support of Hart's independence and to lessen the nutrition of an extreme reaction to his perceived helplessness.

So I re-wrote the empowerment script by fortifying the opportunities for success – catalogued appropriately as Kodak Moments – when things are positive and on-track:

"Wow, Hart. I see you struggling a bit and frustrated, but you are still trying and you are breathing deeply to stay calm. That's so powerful!"

"Hart, you are not yelling or throwing your pencil with this upset! You are sitting and trying again. That is powerful control and persistence. You are being successful!"

"Hart, keep up the great effort of reading the directions and thinking about what you are reading! You ARE doing this yourself!" (This is one of my personal favorites).

Nowadays, pleas for a reduced consequence represent the final frontier I face. Hart baits me with his attempts to forego a consequence for breaking a rule: "Just one more chance, Mom; I can do it with one more chance." Blaming Hart for honing his skills and hitting my weak spot isn't productive for either of us. He's just trying to get what he wants. Don't we all want to get what we want? Goal-directed persistence is a major success marker in life. So my current script goes something like this (and believe me, I need a script when I'm wobbly in those intense moments of sugar sweet testing from my powerful warrior/teacher/son):

"Another chance isn't really fair to you, Hart. It's unclear and we all need things to be clear."

"Reminders allow us to forget you can really do it the first time with no reminders."

"I don't want to insult our intelligence or wisdom with changing something that is already working, even if each of us wants a change sometime."

"You are too smart and powerful for second chances on rule breaks."

And my personal favorite: "You are truly in your power when things are clear. That's why the rules don't change."

Consequences are short and sweet these days – just a minute or less in duration. Hart chose to rename consequences 'resets.' He clearly understands them as a means to "reset his power" (our words at home). Hart is learning quickly to regain his self-control these days. Sometimes the negative tide is strong in its pull and he resists a reset. When Hart refuses, I say: "That's fine. Your privileges will be available as soon as you complete the reset you owe." Never once has he refused for more than a few hours to complete it.

Sometimes my husband, Glenn, and I lapse into the old paradigm territory we grew up with – removing privileges. It doesn't really work. Taking away privileges Hart really loves for misbehaviors is just a short-term solution, which isn't really a solution at all. Responding to the injustice of it, Hart feels deprived and furious for the unpredictable loss. So far, I haven't found any teachable moments within that emotional state or type of consequence for our son.

What has worked with much more significance for major rule breaks beyond the usual reset (like hitting us or extreme disrespect) is community service. The last time Hart hit me, he owed me one hour of community service in the garden. He worked for over 30 minutes alone outside in the winter rain. In the process, I filled him up with increased recognitions for persistence, attention to detail, doing hard work in the rain, making our garden more beautiful, and showing his helpful spirit. It became a consequence with teachable moments and clear evidence of his productive power.

Our parental warrior directive now is to offer him his day's-end review of all the "I can" successes he displayed. We highlight prime examples of Hart's adequacy and ability, his unique worth, powerful strengths and fantastic choices throughout the day. There's not a more satisfying way to end a tough day full of life's lessons.

So, the work of a Yoga mom with shades of 'sergeant benevolence' is moment by moment. The job is at times thankless, but deeply gratifying. I'm thankful I've held my ground against the will of the moment, in support of Hart's highest place; thankful I've bathed his spirit in the warmth and shine of the day's positive highlights. Nothing is sweeter than his small warrior hand (without a sword) reaching out at bedtime, offering to me another kiss and to both of us his own most powerful medal of commendation: "I really CAN do it, Mom!"

Jennifer Easley is a Master's level Counselor, nationally and state certified with specialty certifications in child and elder mental health. She is the co-author of *Transforming the Difficult Child*. Twenty years of working with difficult children could not prepare her for the emotional mountains and spiritual growth realized through parenting her own warrior-child.

It was so much fun reading this with baited breath four or five years after this incident. I actually clearly remember the visit, but only vaguely remembered the details, and failed to remember what I said or did. So I was as curious as anyone in reading this.

I totally love that this sharing of Jenn's process is uncensored and inclusive of all the emotions and all the aborted attempts to respond to Hart. Jenn has the greatness of revealing her process for all to prosper from as well as the greatness of arriving at a place of wonderful clarity and resolution.

I couldn't agree with her more that this process of going through the fire with a child, in this case an amazingly intense child, is what brings one to yet greater and greater levels of revelation and discovery. I do share with Jenn the belief that parent-child struggles of this nature are a perfect vehicle for bringing forth the highest levels of attainment for the parents and the child – that is, if you eventually find an approach that serves that purpose. Hopefully for all reading this book, the Nurtured Heart Approach serves you well in this endeavor.

I should really tell my side of Jenn's story here. When I opened my clinic in Tucson, which existed from 1995 until 1999, Jenn had just moved there and was introduced by a great mutual friend as a therapist who might be perfect to be part of this work. It happened to work out and happened that she was essentially better at the Nurtured Heart Approach than I was within a matter of four hours of training and within a matter of days of putting it into practice.

When Jenn relocated the next year because of her husband's work, I was struggling with writing of my first book, Transforming the Difficult Child. *Since I already knew of her great writing style and her great flair for this work, it was perfect that she was available to 'midwife' the approach into a literary style, which essentially delivered this yet unknown approach to the world. Jenn is the person who made that happen. The book might still be in unedited pieces on my desk if not for her.*

And then a few short years later, this incredible being named Hart Easley arrives onto the scene. What a gift to the planet he is. His creative juices know no bounds. His life force is compelling and amazing. How ironic that he pressed Jenn's already great talents to the max in order to find the energetic level of Nurtured Heart that matched his needs.

It always will entail finding just the right trajectory of creating and delivering evidence of success, greatness and inner wealth. And it will always entail finding and delivering the level of consequences that matches the child's perception of what level of clarity he needs. This, of course, is always integrally linked with the child's perception of receiving/not receiving energy, relationship and closeness in connection with negativity.

This story couldn't illustrate this any better. It is a masterpiece that is a tribute to two parents experimenting with eyes open and allowing frustration and experience to eventually lead to the iteration that best serves their child. I applaud the greatness of Jennifer and Glenn Easley – specifically the greatness of warrior-like intention, the greatness of perseverance and determination, and the greatness of creativity and power, qualities that go together like five fingers on a hand poised for getting things done. **HNG**

SECTION IV:
EXPANDING THE HEALING VISION

This section of the book is devoted to the stories we have received that do not necessarily illustrate one of the three Stands of the Nurtured Heart Approach. Instead, they are examples of many other ways people have applied and had successes with the approach. We hope they prompt you to consider ways you might also be able to creatively use the approach to help your loved ones, or even yourself, bring out the greatness and inner wealth each of us possesses inside.

Howard Glasser and Jennifer Easley

A Nurtured Heart Poem

By Bryan Forney,
Christina Kappen
and Tracy Krebs

I came down the stairs today and what did I see.
Little Johnny was drawing a picture of me.
First, I wanted to correct his inaccurate picture.
And started into a rambling lecture.
Then a vision of Howard Glasser came rushing through my mind.
And I knew that pointing out what I observed is more kind.
So I started noticing what he was doing.
By pointing out that he was cutting and gluing.
I continued to notice what he was saying and feeling.
And much to my surprise, Johnny starting smiling.
I didn't pass judgment on Johnny's creation.
I just noticed the detail in a tone of admiration.
I sensed what was forming was a deeper relationship.
As Johnny ran out to play with a hop and a skip.

Cindy Skinner, who submitted this poem, is Executive Director of Focus on Youth in Cincinnati, where they use Nurtured Heart Approach in their work with foster families. They have developed a curriculum for training foster parents in the approach and currently are working on an internal certification process to certify their families as 'Nurtured Heart families,' a highly regarded designation that will be useful in matching children in need to foster homes. She believes the approach has transformed children, replacing despair with hope. She credits her "incredible, high-energy and committed staff" including Kim Brown and poem co-authors Bryan Forney, Christina Kappen and Tracy Krebs.

───────────── ☙ ─────────────

This poem was created as part of a 'Focus on Youth' staff train-
ing experience. It came from the hearts of Bryan, Christina and
Tracy as they empathetically imagined into new ways to be with
and support a high energy/challenging child. It was contributed
by Cindy Skinner, the Executive Director of Cincinnati's Focus
on Youth. It is a beautiful commentary on how the old para-
digm of judging and correcting must surrender to a new means
of relationship-building and calling forth a child's greatness.

Deep gratitude to Cindy for fostering a new vision to support our youth and to Bryan, Christina and Tracy for offering their transformation poem and front-line support to our young future leaders! JLE

What a fantastic depiction of a reset by this brilliant team doing extraordinary work in the field of foster care. This poem shows the simplicity and beauty of remembering to move the conversation to appreciation and success rather than criticism and correction – even if it takes conjuring up an image of me! By taking the stance to foster positive relationship, these caregivers inspired Johnny to relax into the joy and greatness that I believe is there for the 'igniting' in every child. HNG

5:30 A.M.: Time for a Transformation of No Return

By Tom Grove

This is about my own personal recognition of the power of this approach. I had been in the Nurtured Heart advanced training for two days but just wasn't experiencing the fire others seemingly were. Many participants were loaded with stories of joy and success, but it still sounded like 'grandma's love' to me. I awoke at 5:30 a.m. the third day, my mind racing with thoughts of all the negative things my son had NOT done that he easily could have: things that would have gotten him in deep trouble, messed up his hope for the future, wounded his heart, labeled him a failure in his own mind, stunted his strength of will, filled him with regrets, twisted his spirit, made him an outcast, or put him on a list with the law.

In those moments, I realized he had actively chosen to direct his life in ways I never appreciated. He had just been doing what he should do and was being a good son. He was like a great car or machine that ran very well and was reliably and consistently doing what it was made to do. Even though I truly loved him, I had taken his positive choices for granted.

Suddenly and with a force I will never forget, he became a very different son and I became a very different father. I was 1,100 miles from him, yet felt as if I was with him more deeply and closely and in more ways than ever. He was much more alive, mature, real, individual, loved, appreciated, respected, vivid, soulful, deep of spirit, wisely strong-willed, thoughtful, patient, dedicated, loving, sacrificing, self-controlled; in other words, so much more than I could have hoped for.

I was filled with regret that I had never appreciated him with the depth of clarity I now had, yet joyful that I had suddenly unearthed that clarity to lavish on him. Our past times together ran like a movie – both familiar yet totally new in the light of my transformed awareness of him. Never again would he just be the good son doing what he should do. Henceforth, I would recognize that he was always choosing that goodness over and over. And I would never again merely be the good father just doing what he should do. I had some celebrating to do, some recognition of my son's character and spirit to catch up on, and a vastly deeper love to share him. It is 5:34 a.m., the transformation is complete.

Tom Grove, since that moment of transformation, has poured his heart into making our schools places of transformation for all children. He and Howard Glasser co-wrote *The Inner Wealth Initiative: The Nurtured Heart Approach for Educators* with Melissa Block. It is an inspiring guide for propelling transformation in schools to help all educators and administrators bring forth the greatness in our youth.

--------------------- ❦ ---------------------

Tom's 5:30 a.m. download of personal, life-changing awareness is a deep teaching to all parents. He so eloquently and truthfully offers us the moments we, too, have missed recognizing and honoring our children's greatness. It is, as Tom says, the place of no returning to an ordinary view of our children's greatness taken for granted. What a deeply fortunate and powerful son Tom must have – to be both the catalyst for his father's transformation as well as the already amazing recipient! Deep gratitude to Tom for sharing this personal, 'no turning back' stellar moment of father consciousness. JLE

Tom's depiction of all that can transpire in the course of four minutes is stunning. To me it reveals not only the great capacity the heart has to forge new horizons, but the blurring speed at which the heart can accomplish such feats of vastness.

I happen to remember Tom sitting in that advanced training, appearing to be bored to tears in response to a track I took that seemed relatively unproductive at the time. Little did I know that he was percolating a new dimension that would ultimately be a major contribution to the world – and one that continues to grow and grow.

I believe the true nature of Tom's revelation came from seeing one central point of the Nurtured Heart Approach – that the absence of problems is a powerful vantage point that we can superimpose upon any given moment to use as a valid and true measure of success. The fact that his son was gliding through life without creating disturbances and challenging issues can beg the question (one that Tom is fond of asking now): "What does that say about his greatness?"

I am so thrilled to know that Tom can now approach his son frequently with the answer to that question with statements such as, "Warren, I really appreciate the greatness you show when you stay focused on your graduate studies – you have great diligence and determination." With Tom's creativity in seeing the beauty of his son and the beauty of the opportunity of the moment, there is no end to the great things he can deliver to the heart of his child.

Due in large part to this early morning awakening Tom experienced, he has catapulted to having an enormous impact on so many schools and educators across the country. In 2006 he co-authored The Inner Wealth Initiative, *bringing the Nurtured Heart Approach further into the world of education. And he continues to bring this blazing attunement, and his great gift of knowledge and brilliance, to the faculty of Advanced Trainings. HNG*

Life Is Like a Peach Pit

By Gretchen Martin

Karen Wassmann and I have been neighbors for about 11 years, attend the same AA self-help group and are like family. Karen introduced me to the Nurtured Heart Approach of parenting, so I began to use it with my son. I didn't realize it at the time, but I was teaching Karen, too. The whole answer to life is love and self-responsibility. The Nurtured Heart Approach is a self-help program. You can learn to point with love.

My mother and I always had problems as I was growing up, so when I became a mother, I had to have a perfect child to show my mother how good I was. Unfortunately, my son was difficult from the beginning – I even hit the doctor when my son was born because his birth was so difficult! David threw tantrums, was rebellious and very negative. I tried everything: spanking, yelling, sending him to his room, and denying TV privileges. I have a particularly painful memory from early motherhood. During a visit by my mother, I was so angry giving my son a spanking, my mother made me quit in the middle of the spanking for fear I would hurt him. Those were the dark days.

My husband Bob was a Police Lieutenant, so loved by both of us. Bob pampered David. His unexpected death as a young man, when David was just a teen, was a blow to both of us. Other losses happened for Dave as well. He returned from service in the Navy with both drug and alcohol involvement. He married, but his wife was also drug addicted, and they divorced. I found faith after my husband died, but not before going through a dark night of the soul. I resumed heavy drinking after years of sobriety. Now I see this dark time as ultimately having a positive outcome. I'm actually glad I got drunk enough to get some help.

David and I also tried therapy but ended up leaving our one and only appointment feeling shamed and blamed for the problems between us. Finally, for many years, my son and I just did not speak to each other.

Things began to change when David moved in with me about 10 years ago. I was having troubles due to dizziness and falling, and I needed a caretaker. He was divorced and without a place to live. Despite our adult status, it was a difficult adjustment, and I again found my now adult son being very contrary. I began looking at the Nurtured Heart principles as a way to perhaps heal this gulf between us. Now, I don't blame him for everything that goes wrong. I've learned the power of love and focusing on the positives I see that he does.

David is now 63 and I am 96. These days, I do more laughing and admitting I might be wrong about things. The Nurtured Heart Approach has helped me lighten up! When I think about words of wisdom to share with others who are struggling with intense or challenging children, I would tell them to reflect on what they can change about themselves, not the other person. I have tried to be controlling in the past, especially as a new mother. My biggest challenges were recognizing my controlling attitude, not reacting when David or I failed to meet my standards, and realizing I can control only myself, not him or anyone else.

I have calmed down. I have learned patience, tolerance and acceptance – and it doesn't mean I have to like something. I now understand that I have chosen both the light and the darkness of what I've done. It's up to me to react or not react. Faith in the power of love and in my Higher Power has solved all my problems. I have learned to live in the moment and not dwell in the past. Now I know I can learn from everything that happens. The most important word is love and to be able to use love every day and every minute of your life.

When I think about the Nurtured Heart Approach and my life, I am reminded of a writing given to me by my AA sponsor, Dorothy. It's about life being like a peach pit.

Who in their life hasn't planted a peach pit.
Just hoping that somehow a seedling would grow.
And then they move on to some other adventure.
And if it comes up, well they don't even know.
That's one way of picturing your style of living.
You've planted ideas and dreams unaware.
You've noticed somebody whose heart needs attention and planted
     a positive feeling in there.
It's part of your nature.

You may not remember the kind and encouraging things that you've done.

But everywhere 'peach pits' are growing like crazy, and people are blooming.

I know it – I'm one.

Gretchen celebrated her 96th birthday recently and reluctantly. She shares her wisdom from many years as a recovered alcoholic and a mother who has seen the transformations of the Nurtured Heart Approach, even with her live-in son, who is now in his 60s. Gretchen credits the approach as one of the main reasons she and her son are speaking today. She also credits her Higher Power for the transformations in their relationship. "My Higher Power is as close as a heart beat and as far away as the stars, but if I can look at a person lovingly, it makes my day."

It was thoroughly delightful and illuminating to speak with Gretchen several times by phone when she was in the process of sharing this amazing story of her lifetime and use of the Nurtured Heart Approach. I felt deeply graced and held by the passion and compassion of Gretchen, who is a firecracker bursting forth with love, wisdom and insight that comes from moving through deep losses gracefully, with conviction rooted in deep faith. Still full of vim and vigor, fueled by the energy and resolve of loving transformations of self and family, Gretchen is a flowing spring of awareness for some really hard life lessons and losses. She never gave up on herself and her son, and because of this, they are living greater realities of acceptance and harmony within their family.

Gretchen's story is the one we need to hear. She reminds us it's never too late, the child is never too old, and the parent never beyond hope – especially in the wise, golden years of majesty. Deep gratitude to you, Gretchen, for sharing with us your wise woman pearls from a lifetime of living, seeking and loving! May we all be so wise! JLE

This story is particularly meaningful to me, having lost my own elderly mother recently and having been aware for so long that relationships are precarious and precious; they can be damaged and even lost because of the squirrelly parent and child conflicts that can ensue given the realities of an intense and challenging child. It's one of the reasons that I've been so passionate about my work. Having personally experienced those conflicts and estranged relationship for years with my Mom, I feel like part of what I am fighting for in my work is helping parents recover and move farther than ever into a realm of enjoyment and closeness in their connection.

It then is amazing that Gretchen took it upon herself to find a way to remedy the situation – by planting seeds of appreciation and positivity. And she also clearly found for herself a spiritual way and rationale for resetting. The Alcoholics Anonymous serenity prayer is a marvelous metaphor for not giving energy to negativity – for having the discerning ability to choose to not give energy where energy would only fuel the old fire. This was such a perfect fix for all that had separated her from Dave in the past and that drove them farther apart.

Lastly, it pains me that, in seeking help, this mom and son actually felt shamed and blamed. Unfortunately, that so easily becomes a sidebar to therapy methods that seek to solve problems by exploring the roots of problems. I hope this story goes a long way to demonstrate that there is an alternative way to accomplish a great outcome – a peach of a way. *HNG*

The Wise Woman Next Door

By Karen Wassmann

Gretchen is my 96-year-old neighbor whom I've known for 20 years, and she has been an inspiration to me through all that time. Gretchen has been my spiritual mentor. She has taught me to live my life according to spiritual principles. Her support and teachings have helped me gracefully weather the ups and downs of ordinary life. Her most important contribution to my spiritual development was her modeling the value of living according to the spiritual tenants of the Twelfth Step program of Alcoholics Anonymous – love being the primary source and guiding force in all relationships.

Despite the wonderful person Gretchen was, she continually had problems with her adult son who lived with her. She was doing what most parents do when trying to correct undesirable behaviors in their children: giving a lot of negative energy to their inappropriate behavior. Her intentions to correct undesirable behavior in her son were laudable. But they backfired. Such strategies strengthened and supported the unwanted behavior by deepening her son's impression that he got more energized relationship through poor choices. Gretchen was in a common parental rut.

It was painful to watch how such a wise and enlightened woman with so much love in her heart could not find a way to reach and help her difficult adult son. And I, a trained clinical social worker specializing in helping children and their families, was unable to help. These were my friends, not my clients, so traditional therapy was out of the question. Help came in an unexpected way: Nurtured Heart Approach to the rescue.

As a counselor for emotionally handicapped children at a Miami-Dade public school, I and my daughter Tessy Wassmann, who is a school counselor at a private school in Miami, attended an advanced training workshop by Howard Glasser on the Nurtured Heart Approach. Gretchen's son certainly met the criteria for difficult, and Howie's approach shed light on Gretchen's dilemma. She was doing what Howie says parents often do – inadvertently energizing (and thereby stimulating) her son's unwanted behavior. Gretchen needed to redirect her energy to reward positive behavior in her son.

211

By the end of the workshop, Tessy and I knew "what to do and how to do it" in order to help Gretchen. We also knew that the Nurtured Heart Approach was compatible with our psychological training, clinical experience and spiritual beliefs.

Tessy and I were eager to try out this approach in our own family. The results were amazing. Our own relationships with our children were enriched and the children excelled. We confirmed that the approach applies not only to transforming difficult children, but also to helping ordinary children excel. We tried the approach with our clients and the results were equally amazing. Children behaved better and the relationships between parents and children were much stronger.

To teach Gretchen the Nurtured Heart concepts, we began with the story of the toll-booth attendant to illustrate the importance of perception. It helped her see her son in a different light. She was able to see what he was already doing that was appropriate and celebrate his achievements. The Shamu story helped her understand the importance of modifying her expectations of her son so that she would be able to create many opportunities to nurture him and foster a pattern of success. Gretchen could now create experiences of success for her son no matter how difficult his behavior became; there was always a behavior that could be rewarded. Gretchen took to the approach like a duck to water. She also applied the AA tenet 'progress not perfection.' In other words, any application of the Nurtured Heart strategies, even if it's not 100 percent of the time, will promote considerable gains in the relationship and in creating inner strength in the other person.

Consequently, lowering the bar (her expectations) was a crucial strategy that enabled her to praise and nurture her son for the things he could do, rather that focus on those things he could not do. She was able to take charge of her relationship with him and create experiences of success for him that would not otherwise exist.

Results were astonishing. Rapport between them increased. In addition, the knowledge that she could always start over in applying the strategies, even after a lapse or sense of failure, was also very important for Gretchen.

Furthermore, Gretchen was able to nurture herself, applying the Nurtured Heart concepts to herself while learning the new way of interacting with her son. She learned to focus on what she was able to do and feel pride in her accomplishments. She learned to redirect her thinking, both about her son and herself, to a more positive channel. Taking stock of her progress was another way that she applied the program to herself and her son. It has been very gratifying to watch Gretchen and her son transform.

In my professional capacity, I have been blessed by witnessing amazing transformations of difficult children. It has also been wonderful to witness ordinary children flourish when raised with the approach. Moreover, I have gained a great deal of satisfaction from teaching the Nurtured Heart Approach. In classrooms the outcomes have been very positive. Children are happier and teachers more empowered. My experience is that it works with oneself and others regardless of age, circumstances or gender. My belief is that Nurtured Heart is truly a spiritual approach that builds competency and inner wealth in whomever directs and whomever receives its nourishment.

Karen Wassmann is a Certified Nurtured Heart Specialist in private practice. She specializes in training parents/teachers in behavioral management strategies for the prevention and treatment of behavioral problems in children. Her daughter Tessy Wassmann has a Master's in Counseling and currently works as a college counselor for the Gulliver Pinecrest Preparatory School.

What a beautiful seed of mutual support and sweetness has been blooming in this Florida neighborhood! Neighbors like Gretchen, Karen and Tessy who nurture and support each other in ways that call forth individual and community healing – are a rare and precious commodity. Karen offers a lovely glimpse of what happens when she and Gretchen cared enough about each other to invest time in each other's growth and lives.

I loved how Karen offered the toll booth and Shamu stories as teachings to reach a dear friend in pain. Karen's story reminds us that sharing our stories can be the road to heart and healing and that "family" can extend well beyond our front doors. Thank you, Karen and Tessy, for sharing Nurtured Heart with Gretchen and with those whose lives you touch professionally as well. JLE

You can almost feel the glee of Karen and Tessy in recounting the journey they took in bringing the Nurtured Heart Approach to Gretchen. I love how they systematically introduced her to the thinking of the approach and then the process, how they supported her in using it, and how they eventually led her to using the approach in a self-directed way as well. Once Gretchen 'got it,' she was an unstoppable force. That is precisely why it means so much to me to introduce the approach in the way Tessy and Karen describe their process – in a way that truly makes sense to the heart and mind. In my experience, once it makes sense, then the person can virtually reinvent the approach in a way that fits their style.

Even a 60-something-year-old son needs a parent's appreciation and limits (spouses, too, for that matter), and this story unfolds the pieces of that puzzle so beautifully. I am so appreciative of how these friends have lent such great support to one another. Yea Miami NHA – much preferred to Miami VICE in my way of thinking! **HNG**

Changing History's Course in One Generation

By Karen Ellis

Siblings Tom and Nancy were placed in the Los Angeles County foster care system because their Aunt Gloria, their primary caregiver, had thrown in the towel. It was my job to work clinically with the kids and the aunt in order to try to get them successfully reunited and the kids out of foster care.

At first, things weren't going well at all. Both kids came with histories including oppositional defiance, poor attitudes, poor school performance, several foster care placements and some suicidal ideations with psychiatric hospitalizations. Their aunt always seemed overwhelmed by them and focused only on the negative behaviors they displayed. Based on their history, she was expecting failure. Overwhelmed and frustrated, she felt like she had few tools to work with in making this placement successful.

I decided to use the Nurtured Heart Approach, both teaching it to Gloria as well as using it in my interactions with her. As a young woman without children of her own, and having grown up in the 'system' herself, she needed to fill up on her own greatness before she was able to alter her perception of her niece and nephew. I gently challenged her perception of her inability to manage difficult situations. I referred to her own experience growing up in the foster care system to show her that she had great strength, courage, and resiliency. Soon thereafter, she was able to see the same attributes in her niece and nephew, and she began to overtly recognize and energize them as well. This determined young woman read the book cover-to-cover and refers to it often when she feels a leak of negativity springing forth. She states that she's a totally different person and, having had the honor of witnessing the transformation, I would agree. Her perceptions of both herself and the kids have changed so much. Now, she is genuinely enjoying her new role as parent and auntie.

In addition, Tom and Nancy report a deep and loving relationship with their aunt. The 'history' that followed them has virtually disappeared. They are doing well in school, have gained their aunt's trust, and are thriving in the home. Overall, their relationships have flourished and they feel like 'normal' kids.

As a transformed agent of change herself now, Gloria's favorite aspect is that she became the 'therapist' – she was able to overcome her dependence on a system where everything was defined through 'problems.' This now empowered young woman says that she wishes this approach was around when she was in foster care. Recognizing and claiming her own courage, strength and abilities allowed Gloria to lead the way to changing the course of history for herself and these lucky children – in just one generation.

Karen Ellis is a licensed family therapist with a small private practice in California who is passionate about bringing peace and joy into the hearts and souls of children and their families through the principles of the Nurtured Heart Approach. She currently is striving to bring Nurtured Heart to public mental health programs.

———————————————— ✿ ————————————————

My deep gratitude to Karen for her brilliant work. I have always found foster parenting one of those things in life that impresses me to the core. It is so amazing that people take non-biological children into their lives and homes and then strive to do every-thing possible to assist them in flourishing.

I applaud Karen's tactic of demonstrating to this new mom that she was already doing much that was successful and build-ing on that. That is precisely the way to go, and I love that this mom was then able to pass the gift of success on to her niece and nephew.

The Nurtured Heart Approach is so applicable to foster care, which makes me love this story all the more. These are children who most often have had such tremendous loss and hardship in their lives already. Then they usually face even more trauma by way of broken and failed placements simply because the foster parents only know how to parent using conventional approaches, which typically do not stand a chance with intense and chal-lenging children. The Nurtured Heart Approach was partially derived from my work with foster parents and children such as these. It is purposely designed to have the power to shift the child to a new life of success and greatness. There are now many foster care agencies in this country and in England exclusively relying on the Nurtured Heart Approach. In fact, one large agency in New Jersey recently reported zero broken placements in the year 2007, compared with 20% or higher in years prior to discovering how well this approach helped them optimize their efforts.

Congratulations to Karen and this transformed family and to the great people everywhere doing foster care. *HNG*

Karen's profound story of the change that transpired in this family ruthlessly defies so much that has been negatively scripted in the mental health and foster care realms. How wise of Karen to know that no headway could be made until Aunt Gloria herself realized her own inner wealth. She employed a masterful means of acknowledging the gifts and strengths gained from the aunt's painful history as evidence and proof of the capabilities she possessed to change the lives of these children (versus proof it wouldn't work – as many professionals believe). I believe this shows that long-term therapy is not necessarily the best means for such deep and complete intergenerational change.

Karen's gem of a story is evidence that our already capitated mental health and foster care dollars would be better spent nurturing inner strength for parents/foster parents as the vital key to empower change and break negative cycles of abuse, poverty and victimization. Blessings to you, Karen! JLE

The Nurtured Heart Crossing

By Gregory J. Boyce

In January 2007, I was leaving Canada for Howard Glasser's week-long Nurtured Heart training in Tucson by way of Toronto International Airport. I needed to pass through U.S. customs and immigration. It had been about six years since the immediate pandemonium of 9-11, after which there were new policies and procedures for Canadians entering the U.S. Some tiny voice inside me was telling me that maybe the word 'training' had become a red flag. When my turn came to approach the security officer, I observed him to be about 35, handsome, fit and sporting a spotless uniform with knife-edge creases – and behind him were back-up personnel in military stances. I'll refer to him as 'The Man.' Here's what transpired during about 45 minutes of interrogation.

The Man: *Place of birth and citizenship.*

Nervous Me: *Canada and Canadian.*

The Man: *Passport and boarding pass.*

Nervous me hands them over.

The Man: *Destination.*

Nervous Me: *Tucson.*

The Man: *Purpose and duration of your trip.*

Nervous Me: *Business* (notice I don't say training), *eight days.*

The Man: *What kind of business.*

Nervous Me: *Parenting conference.*

The Man: *You're in the parenting business.*

Nervous Me: *I work as a psychotherapist, which often means I coach people on parenting issues.*

The Man: *You have a business card.*

Nervous me hands one over.

The Man: *So what's this conference all about exactly.*

Nervous Me: *It's a technique called the Nurtured Heart Approach.*

The Man: *Uh huh, go on.*

Nervous Me: *What we've noticed is that children respond well to parental recognition of all the behaviors they do on an ongoing basis that comply with parent values and rules; yet parents hardly ever give enough of that recognition. So the Nurtured Heart Approach helps parents give children lots of recognition.*

The Man: *You mean praise.*

Nervous Me: *Sort of.*

The Man: *Isn't that over-indulging them.*

Nervous Me [I was shocked and astounded that he'd listened and actually had an appropriate question, so I temporarily forgot what was at stake and replied]: *Here's an example. I've been watching you perform your tasks with me. You've been appropriately polite but serious, giving excellent eye contact, dutifully moving through your checklist, managing the computer and me at the same time. This tells me you are well-trained, skilled, responsible and have an ethical foundation for your work. The fact that you listened to my explanation of the Nurtured Heart Approach and had a thoughtful question also tells me you are present to the situation and fully* *engaged – also admirable qualities. Now, does what I just said feel like over-indulgence?*

The Man gave me some serious eye contact without a smile at first, then the corners of his mouth started to turn up. In a couple of seconds he had a warm smile on his face and, maybe I imagined it, a twinkle in his eye. He handed my passport back (keeping my business card) and said, "Have a nice day, sir."

The moral of the story is that all people, young and old, like to be recognized, to be seen and heard, and are worthy of being seen and heard. I guess another lesson is that I no longer treat my entries into the U.S. as merely crossing a bridge.

Gregory Boyce is a Canadian psychotherapist and Certified Nurtured Heart Specialist who discovered the power of the approach at a most challenging crossing point during his travels.

––––––––––––––––––––––– ☙ –––––––––––––––––––––––

I laughed out loud with delight and deep satisfaction at Gregory's unexpected crossing story. It was comically cathartic, especially given the potentially dire stakes. Gregory might well never have made it to the advanced training had he not been a master of Recognitions and Appreciations! Although most of us may never use the Nurtured Heart Approach to melt the steely heart of authority, as Gregory so gracefully did, it's fabulous to know it works in such a serious situation.

Although curiously tempted to use Gregory's tact the next time I'm pulled over for a traffic infraction, it's comforting to know that behind every uniform of authority, responsibility and seeming rigidity lies a heart just waiting to be seen and nurtured! Three cheers and deep chuckles for Gregory Boyce, our creative Canadian transformer. JLE

In addition to this being a great story from a most entertaining man (I've heard Gregory tell it in person), this is a most amazing example of how utterly powerful it is to be appreciative of another in the detailed manner that we use in this approach. Gregory demonstrates irrefutably to this officer that he has been seen and admired as well as applauded for the qualities of greatness in how he conducted himself. By doing so, Gregory instantly created positive relationship – not just any relationship, but relationship that will undoubtedly affect this man forever.

Gregory demonstrates that, if you are keenly attuned to what IS in the moment, then you not only are able to acknowledge that to another, but the recipient really prospers from hearing the message of how wonderful he or she is. And the beauty is that there are always wonderful things to acknowledge by tuning yourself in on that level. This type of interaction always seems to instantly transport the giver and the receiver of that message to their hearts – and that seems to be where spirit resides.

So glad Gregory made it over the border to that training. What an inspiring therapist he is and what a great contribution he makes to his community. HNG

From Difficult to Delightful

By Tami Gulland

For many years I enjoyed a successful career as a marketing consultant and manager. My career path and interest changed when my husband and I had our first child. We learned much from the school of life with our son, Grant, as one of the main teachers.

In truth, as a mother I wasn't prepared for my son's intensity. From the time Grant was 18 months old, he was hyperactive and difficult. It quickly became apparent to my husband and me that our friends couldn't relate to having a highly energized child or our situation. We felt very isolated and frustrated. Struggle seemed to be our theme. I so wanted to have a peaceful and happy family. I WANTED to enjoy parenting, only I knew that I wasn't. For us, frustration became a powerful motivator for change.

So I delved into many approaches to help Grant balance his energy and calm his disposition. My attempts included supplements, homeopathy, chiropractic care, natural allergy elimination treatments, participation in a special study with a stringent diet, elimination of all food coloring and additives, an anti-yeast diet, detoxification for heavy metals that were found in his body, at least two popular parenting approaches, and the list goes on.

At one point, when my son was 5 years old, I took him to the family doctor for a food sensitivities blood test. He took one look at our son and diagnosed him with kinesthetic ADD, recommending a low dose of medication until he was 9 or 10, which I refused. The doctor also suggested I consider home schooling if I wanted my son's 'throttle to be left wide open.' He felt that the traditional school setting would result in trauma for Grant. In other words, Grant was a kinesthetic learner – one that takes in and expresses life through his body. Teachers in the traditional school setting typically teach to auditory and visual learners. For Grant, sitting in his chair was the equivalent of a visual learner being blindfolded or an auditory learner wearing earplugs. Grant didn't 'fit into the box' at school.

Many of the strategies we employed with Grant contributed to varying degrees of improvements in our son's behavior. Still, something was missing as we continued to be challenged by his behavior. His younger sister had started to become Grant's understudy and the pressure was on for us to find a solution before the problems multiplied.

On a late-night Internet search, I discovered a book entitled *Transforming the Difficult Child: The Nurtured Heart Approach*. I ordered it, knowing intuitively my son would flourish with the approach. My husband and I began to implement the approach immediately. Nothing we had done with our son up to that point was as dramatic and transformational. We went from surviving to thriving. I'm not going to kid you – it did take commitment and some work. But the results were far more amazing than I could have guessed.

I was so inspired by the transformation of our son that I went on to personally train with Howard Glasser, creator of the Nurtured Heart Approach, in addition to completing other family coach training. Thus my new career as a family coach unfolded. I realized that if my husband and I were struggling (and I consider us intelligent, caring people), there were probably plenty more parents who were struggling, too. I wanted to help them achieve the calmer, closer family they desire.

Our Beginning

We began the approach at home before Grant entered first grade. It wasn't long before we routinely observed Grant following directions (instead of being defiant), eagerly wanting to help with chores, showing self-control and sharing toys. He even tried to hide some Yugi-O cards under his pillow one night and decided to confess because he recognized lying was breaking the rules, and he didn't want to do that.

Grant was continuing to have problems in school during this time. We asked to implement the approach at school, yet the teacher, guidance counselor, social worker and psychologist decided to pick one problem behavior – Grant sitting in his seat – and work on it with traditional behavior modification. After three months, Grant was continuing to have discipline problems at school. Sensing the situation hadn't improved, I called for an extended parent-teacher meeting. Five school personnel greeted my husband and me at the conference:

three of his teachers, plus a guidance counselor and school psychologist.

After about 45 minutes of listening to each of them discuss Grant's problems and possible solutions like special education and medications, I took my turn. I told the group what we were observing at home. I went through example after example of Grant's positive behavior. I then asked them to help us turn Grant's behavior around at school by using the Nurtured Heart Approach. The three teachers reluctantly agreed, while the guidance counselor and school psychologist were silent.

In less than a month of implementing the approach, each teacher was seeing a vast positive improvement. After three months into the approach at school, which was at the end of first grade, his main teacher told me: "If I didn't know Grant before, I wouldn't have thought it was the same child." His first-grade reading teacher requested Grant be placed in her second-grade class.

Many family members and friends commented on Grant's newfound happiness and success in all areas of his life.

One year later, we continued to witness improved competence with making and keeping friends, social skills, positive decision-making, cooperation and the ability to articulate feelings versus emotional outbursts. Now Grant is the one who recognizes when a friend isn't speaking kind words, isn't taking turns or is interrupting him. And he tells us, "You do things differently than everybody else's parents. Why are they so mean? They could say things nicer. You don't say it that way." Grant articulates his feelings instead of acting them out through negative behavior. Even though telling us what is wrong had been hard for him, we now hear him say things like: "I'm really sad when …" and "I'm really disappointed when…."

We have watched the true essence of our son come forth in beautiful and successful ways. It is like we are getting to really know him for the first time. This is the amazing child who was underneath all the struggles, frustration, emotional outbursts and defiant behavior. This approach has been a gift from God and an answer to our prayers. It is a gift that keeps giving, too.

Off on the Right Foot

Grant burst through the door after his first day of second grade. "I want to work at being better at school and being a better friend," he announced. "Really?" I asked him. "Tell me about that." Grant explained that his teacher had every child write down what they were good at and what they wanted to be better at in second grade. "Those are wonderful things to work toward. What a great way to use your power and ability this year!" I replied.

The Second-Grade Holiday Show

Grant quietly went over to his music teacher during class and said, "I can't stand next to Sam." Sam was trying to get Grant's attention the whole time they were practicing for the class' holiday show. Grant decided, on his own, that this situation just wasn't going to work. He needed to do something since he had a solo part pretending to play a saxophone. He wanted to do a good job. He figured out a solution and, despite being eager to have friends, he took matters into his own hands and stood up for himself. Both his music teacher and later his homeroom teacher told Grant how proud they were of him and his great problem-solving skills. Grant announced to us he deserved 10 extra points on his credit chart for that day. He did indeed earn those extra points. But more importantly, he had greatly increased his inner wealth and the reflection of it to the outside world.

The School Bus Incident

Ever since kindergarten, Grant has had a tumultuous relationship with a peer, Jeb, who rides the same bus as Grant. In kindergarten they were friends. They got into trouble together. They've been in the same class twice. Jeb's choices often land him in the principal's office. In second grade, Grant distanced himself from Jeb. He was seeing the poor choices Jeb makes. One day, Grant came home and said, "Jeb was trying to make me mad on the bus today. He was saying mean things to me." When I asked what Grant did, he said, "Ignored him." I praised him for not letting Jeb upset him. Grant replied, "Why should I? Jeb is a dufus." While I don't condone name-calling, this was certainly discerning of Grant.

More Progress

Grant's physical education teacher reported that Grant was working really hard in second grade and had no complaints with his behavior. Physical Education is now his favorite class. His second-grade teacher was amazed at Grant's huge social and behavioral improvements and the progress he continued to make. His fine motor skills became more refined and writing more legible. He no longer called himself a loser or seeks relationships with others through negative attention. He is calmer and more content with himself and life in general.

Catapulting into Personal Empowerment – Third Grade

The school district in which we live built a new school and rezoned the school district. For third grade, Grant was transferred to the new school with new teachers and principal. In previous years, this transition would have been highly detrimental to Grant's behavior, choices and attitude. Grant, though slightly concerned, was really excited to be attending a new school. He transitioned beautifully and now thinks his school is the best. He set a goal at the beginning of the year to make more friends. He recently reported a running count of 30. He has been invited to more birthday parties, more friends' houses to play and shows much more understanding of the friends, their feelings and being a friend.

At the mid-year parent-teacher conference, his teacher told us that Grant should be very proud of himself for the progress he has made this year. Across the board, all of Grant's teachers were reporting improvements in listening skills, following directions, positive attitude, good participation and effort, self-control and staying on task.

When we received Grant's report card, we were delighted. It was his best report card ever. Mind you, academics were never the issue for Grant. This report card indicated, via a check-minus, two areas of personal development that could use a little work. Grant announced to us that "he was going to have all checks and check-pluses on his next report card." He reached his goal and was ecstatic about his accomplishment.

Grant has proved to himself, over and over, what he is capable of. He prides himself on his cursive writing, creative ideas, math skills, athletic ability and his ability to connect with people. Grant's overall demeanor is much more peaceful, harmonious and content than it was even last year and it continues on! That doesn't mean that he isn't still a high-energy, creative kid. He is! Only now, he is more aware of how he is feeling, is able to express it without acting it out and trusts that we encourage and support him. He now guides his little sister on how to be a good friend, teaches her how to do things and helps her make good choices. Grant told us that when we are busy or frustrated, he goes to his room and begins reading a book. Now that is a transformation.

The Nurtured Hearted Parents

As a parent, the Nurtured Heart Approach changed how I looked at everything. It gave me hope. It gave me inspiration. It gave me a practical tool, a minute-by-minute reminder, to stay focused on positives and gratitude. It doesn't take away all of the issues that can arise but provides the tools to turn the negatives into positives.

The approach changed how we talk to our son and daughter. It changed how I talk to myself and to the others around me, from hotel cleaning staff and teachers to neighbors and my children's friends.

My son and daughter have been two of the greatest teachers I could have hoped for. While all of the lessons have not been easy, they were indeed worthwhile. I'm committed to bringing out the best in my children and all children, and ultimately, in our future. The Nurtured Heart Approach is a powerfully positive way to honor each child for who he or she is, reinforcing through words and action that every child is born for a reason and is here to do great things in their own way.

Tami Gulland mentors parents struggling with intense children to transform their child's life and their relationship through one-on-one sessions, teleclasses, seminars and online resources. Her gift, born out of her own life journey, is transforming people's pain to wisdom and their sense of struggle to empowerment and positive change. Tami and her husband have a 9-year-old son and 5-year-old daughter and live near Madison, Wisconsin.

———————————————— ♨ ————————————————

I love the inspiring joy Tami takes in the transformation of Grant and I love that she connects the dots and sees that his progress at school resulted from her willingness to fight the odds and ask for what she wanted. So many people get railroaded in meetings where the deck is stacked. School psychologists, administrators and teachers can be very powerful people and daunting when they hit what they perceive to be a wall and lose sight of the possibilities. Similarly, many people have a deep trust in the medical community's long-standing opinion that medications are the first and foremost way to go. It takes tremendous courage and clarity to stand up to the 'team' and ask for what you want, which is precisely what these parents did.

Grant's positive changes at home and school would not have happened without use of the approach to the fullest extent. Ultimately Grant deserves so much credit, but so do his parents and his teachers. Even if this approach makes all the sense in the world, it is not going to have an ounce of impact without the adults taking the ball and running with it. Considering how challenging he was, they all could well have given up, but fortunately they didn't.

It is evident that by way of Tami and her husband shining the light of greatness into the eyes of Grant, he has reached a point of wonderful inner wealth and is flourishing. He is not just 'toeing the line,' he is living his life in an entirely renewed manner. He now gets to use his intensity in great and creative ways.

I also love how Tami was so profoundly influenced by the success of Grant that she began seeing the beauty of applying this approach to herself and others. That is the legacy of our difficult children. They are the ones who inspire us to see the world in a different way and inspire us to bring the lessons learned to every aspect of our lives. Congratulations to all involved. **HNG**

We live in a world where educational and healing paradigms have not yet shifted to adequately support our high-octave children. Despite this, Tami's ability to stand as a warrior-mother for what she knew was the right path (against most all professional recommendations) shines forth. Her story reinforces the immense power and consequence of holding to a nurturing structure and a positive lens with deep, abiding faith and persistence.

By believing in and nourishing Grant's integrity and strong positive sense of self, these powerful parents are now gifted back with seeing their amazing son thrive and mentor his younger sister! What a beautiful family legacy unfolding! JLE

The Nurtured Heart Kid

By Lisa Bravo

One day I was in the toy store checkout line with my children when my daughter Danielle's insight taught me an amazing lesson. There was a child in front of us, maybe 3 or 4 years old, with his mother. He had picked up a candy bar from the rack at the checkout and announced that he wanted it. As we braced for the ensuing tantrum, his mother stopped writing her check, knelt down and looked in his eyes while calmly saying, "I need you to put it back. We are not going to buy that." She stood up and resumed making her purchase. The boy looked at the candy with longing eyes and slowly put it back. The mother picked him up, said something appreciative, gave him a hug, and left the store.

Unbeknownst to me, Danielle was closely observing this whole exchange. She looked at me with reverent eyes and said, "That boy's so lucky to be a nurtured heart kid." When I asked what she meant, she looked at me and said, "I could tell that boy really wanted the candy bar, but he used his strong power to do the right thing. He also wanted to respect his mom, so he listened to her. I could see how proud his Mom was when she gave him that big hug." Awed by her insight and brilliance, I told her how much I loved her and thanked her for sharing her wisdom with me. And I secretly thought: how awesome it is to see the world through the eyes of a child.

This mother is gifted by the gifts she, herself, has offered to her daughter — deep awareness and compassion. Danielle is so filled with personal integrity, empathy and her own greatness that she is able to hold a place of astonishing recognition and awareness for another child also on the path to greatness. Thank you, Danielle, for deeply caring about another, for your ability to recognize strong power to do the right thing, for understanding respect for others, and for your ability to share how you feel in the moment. Thank you, proud and committed mother, for not letting this awesome moment go unrecognized! JLE

Dear Danielle, I am in awe of your great insight and perception, your caring heart and the voice you give to what you know and trust to be true. You already are giving your mother so many gifts of love, gratitude and wisdom, qualities that I suspect will continue to abound. Thank you for bringing your great way of being into this world. I trust that your mother will continue to look at your gifts with great awe and amazing respect. HNG

Blueprint for Building Success

By Rebecca Baker

When I attended Howard Glasser's Nurtured Heart advanced training in 2005, I was searching for a new plan – a blueprint for altering difficult behaviors that weren't responding to my tried and true strategies.

As a master-level teacher with over 17 years of experience, I had worked with all kinds of behaviors in children. However, my strategies were falling short in many cases, and I needed to gain new ways of helping the difficult kids as well as the typically developing kids build a blueprint for success. I found what I was searching for in the Nurtured Heart Approach.

Equipped with my new Nurtured Heart toolbox, I took a leap of faith and started implementing it in my Discovery Connection after-school program. A bullying spirit had taken up residence in our after-school site and that was just the spirit I was looking to transform. Difficult kids are professional drama kings and queens. They walk into a room and with x-ray vision scan their surroundings, tap the resources and stir up dramas that pull everyone into their crazy town. Do you know someone like this? They often do this subconsciously; it's simply a pattern that gives them the biggest payoff of energy and attention. The bullies at our after-school site were very efficient at this. We were all desperate for change.

Our blueprint for success included setting clear boundaries, fervently acknowledging the good we saw in each other, creating productive and compelling 'time-in' for all of us, and using unceremonious time-outs when rules were broken. Sounds like standard good practices to manage children, you say. However, the magic of the Nurtured Heart Approach lies in making a conscious choice, in the midst of good and bad, to capture the good, shine light on it, nurture it and watch it grow. It's a lot like gardening.

The bullies could smell my new toolbox and scrutinized me as I proceeded to list our new rules, all of which started with the word "no." I also introduced 'Praise Notes,' which our staff would be writing daily to acknowledge all the great things that were happening at

Discovery Connection. What I remember most about that day was the children's body language when I stated the rules beginning with "no." They sighed with relief and relaxed their shoulders.

We immediately began acknowledging the children for all the wonderful choices they were making, life skills they were offering and rules they were following. This was a huge shift from when all the energy was being drawn to the bullies and what wasn't going right. The bullies were also being acknowledged for all their goodness; we were creating opportunities for them to be successful and use their amazing power and strength in positive ways.

A month or so after we introduced the Nurtured Heart Approach, the children decided they wanted to elect a mayor for our Discovery Connection site. Our staff supported the idea and discussed what makes a good leader. We even had our town's mayor come in as a guest speaker to talk about leadership.

There were three candidates for Discovery Mayor and one of them was a bully. She was desperate for victory and passed out candy and promises in an attempt to buy votes. But all the focus we had placed on determining the good qualities in a successful leader seemed to make the children really look carefully at the options. The bully's power was diminishing. In the end, the bully lost the election. The new mayor was someone the kids felt could be competent and fair. With a bit of help from staff, the new mayor appointed the bully to help with several special projects, like organizing special field trips. The bully's talents were being tapped for positive pursuits.

The Nurtured Heart Approach is now an integral part of daily life at Discovery Connection after-school sites. I regularly train staff to work with all of our children using the blueprint of success. We have seen a multitude of success stories.

I recently was able to share the Nurtured Heart Approach with parents, educators and community members thanks to grant funds our agency obtained from the Child Abuse Prevention License Plate Program funded by 'The Arizona Republic' newspaper and several local funding partners. I also designed a mentorship program utilizing the approach whereby students from an all-girls therapeutic high school would mentor our Discovery Connection kids. Eleven high school students were chosen to mentor 11 Discovery Connection kids. The high school students were difficult kids themselves, mostly from affluent backgrounds, who needed to turn their lives around. After some basic training in Nurtured Heart, they began working with our program's primarily poor and at-risk children. Our goal was to continue transforming not only our children, but also to give these girls positive outlets for their energy and maybe help them find their inner wealth. The high school mentors spent two hours with their Discovery child each visit, energizing the Discovery kids with the blueprint of success. The results were evident to everyone. The children's smiles, relaxed manner and proud stances served as visible indicators of the positive impact that was taking place for them inside and out.

In closing, the Nurtured Heart Approach is much more than a behavior modification program. It is an approach that is directed at the heart of a child. It acknowledges their true spirit and helps children become stronger from the inside out. It can be customized to all ages. I coach my daughter, an in-home childcare provider, to use the Nurtured Heart Approach with the toddlers she cares for with wonderful results. I sought out the approach to help me work more effectively with difficult children and ended up gaining a new positive paradigm in relating to everyone around me, helping me transform as well. I am so grateful to Howard Glasser for developing and sharing the Nurtured Heart Approach with the world.

Rebecca Baker holds a Master's of Education degree. She designs and implements after-school programs and offers training to parents, teachers and community members. She currently serves as Program Manager for Buena Vista Children's Services, a community-based non-profit that addresses children's issues. "My dedication is to guide children in recognizing their unique gifts and helping them find ways to share them with the world."

———————————————————— ✿ ————————————————————

Rebecca and her inspired Buena Vista Children's Services team have more than created a strong web of extended support for at-risk children. They have fostered deep emotional nourishment and success, a wave that is self-perpetuating as it spreads support and appreciation from youth to youth. This healing ripple is moving not only from the inside to the outside of each child's heart, it is now the structure and support for a new fabric of relationships.

Thank you Rebecca and your team for your courageous work as part of our Nurtured Heart family! We send you unlimited 'Praise Slips' for enacting a new, heart-present way of being with and healing a community – the larger work at hand that our world needs! JLE

I immensely appreciate that you honor my work, Rebecca. However, none of what you all have accomplished and will accomplish in the future would have happened without YOUR brilliance and fierce determination. Your clarity of purpose and deep desire to fill the hearts of these children with inner wealth is what is both winning the day and preparing these children for a greater opportunity to shine on in their lives. Some of these children might never have otherwise sensed their greatness if not for the total effort you are mounting. HNG

Life Is a Long Road

By Christopher Hankins (age 10)

Life is a long road.
There are bumps and cracks.
There are parts being torn off.
There are detours to try to stop you dead in your tracks.

But keep going.
There are adventures yet to be discovered.
There are smooth parts.
There are parts that are new and fresh.
Life is a long road.

Christopher Hankins, author of this poem, describes himself as a Nurtured Heart kid.

———————————— ✥ ————————————

Dear Christopher, yours is a great message of hope and faith and inner strength. You couldn't recommend to your readers to keep going unless you believed in yourself and trusted your ability to handle what is ahead. Those are qualities of your greatness. You couldn't perceive what an adventure yet to be discovered is unless you possessed joy and curiosity about what life has to offer. Those, too, are qualities of your greatness. And you couldn't see that there are parts of life that are smooth, new and fresh unless you, even at age 10, had great wisdom for such a young person, along with great perspective and great appreciation for life. And these great qualities will serve you so well along life's road. Congratulations on becoming so great and choosing to share your greatness with others! **HNG**

Christopher's beautiful and ruthlessly real poem says it all. It's no picnic out there, especially for the highly aware, highly sensitive and wise children we now have as blessings, inspirations, teachers and leaders for our world. What an amazing young man he is, to share his deep and wise consciousness with us. I *can only hope that the long road each of us faces is filled with love, appreciation and recognition for all children. We need to have the vision and clarity to see beyond the bumps and cracks — to the adventure — and offer only pearls of sweetness and support when the detours appear. JLE*

CONTRIBUTORS

Baker, Rebecca L. Camp Verde, Arizona. Certified Nurtured Heart Specialist, Master of Elementary Education, Certified K-8 Teacher. (928) 300-7743, rbaker_03@msn.com

Baxter, Michelle. Columbus, Wisconsin. Certified Nurtured Heart Specialist. (920) 623-1099, mdbaxter@charter.net

Boyce, Gregory J. Ontario, Canada. Certified Nurtured Heart Specialist, Master of Arts, Psychotherapist/ Consultant. 877-837-2411 (toll free), www.boyceco.com

Bravo, Lisa M. Phoenix, Arizona. Certified Nurtured Heart Specialist and Advanced Training Faculty (Nurtured Heart Approach), Master of Counseling, Licensed Professional Counselor, Licensed Independent Substance Abuse Counselor, Nationally Certified Counselor. (480) 248-7595, ParentwoRx.com

Crippen, Stephen. Seattle, Washington. Certified Nurtured Heart Specialist, Master of Arts in Social Science, Marriage and Family Therapy, Licensed Marriage and Family Therapist, Clinical Member of American Association of Marriage & Family Therapists. (206) 214-7650, stephen@stephencrippen.com, www.stephencrippen.com

Duncan-Lewis, Dawn. Anacortes, Washington. Certified Nurtured Heart Specialist, Master of Science, Licensed Marriage & Family Therapist, Clinical Member of American Association of Marriage & Family Therapists, Certified Child Mental Health Specialist, Certified School Counselor. (360) 420-0724, dduncanlewis@hotmail.com

Easley, Jennifer L. Vashon Island, Washington. Certified Nurtured Heart Specialist, Master of Arts in Counselor

Education, Nationally Certified Counselor, Licensed Mental Health Counselor. (206) 300-3142, jennifereasley@comcast.net

Ellis, Karen A. Portland, Oregon. Certified Nurtured Heart Specialist, Licensed Marriage and Family Therapist. (909) 210-3384, Kellis@parentsinprogress.org, www.parentsinprogress.org

Greenish, Michele. Switzerland. Certified Nurtured Heart Specialist, Master of Science in Clinical Psychology with specialty in stress management. (+41) (0)32 322 21 43, mleglobe@aol.com

Grove, Tom. Champaign, Illinois. Certified Nurtured Heart Specialist and Advanced Training Faculty (Nurtured Heart Approach), Licensed Marriage and Family Therapist, co-author *The Inner Wealth Initiative: The Nurtured Heart Approach for Educators* (Grove, Glasser & Block, 2007). (217) 714-5089, twgrove@comcast.net

Gulland, Tami K. Madison, Wisconsin. Certified Nurtured Heart Specialist. (608) 850-6437, Tami@TamiGulland.com, www.TamiGulland.com

Harr, Jamie D. Bachelor of Arts in Education, Certified Special Education K-12 Teacher. (360) 856-1562, jharr@esd189.org

Hunter, Jan. Oklahoma City, Oklahoma. Certified Nurtured Heart Specialist, Team Leader at EnergyParenting.com, Discussion Moderator at difficultchild.com. (405) 517-2686, janhunter@nurturinggreatness.net

Jennings, Karen. Berwick, Maine. Certified Nurtured Heart Specialist, Master in Social Work, Licensed Clinical Social Worker, Animal Assisted Therapy Practitioner. (207) 698-4465

LaChiara, Gabrielli. Amhurst, Massachusetts. Certified Nurtured Heart Specialist and Advanced Training Faculty (Nurtured Heart Approach), Licensed Social Worker. (413) 256-0064, www.gabrielli.org

Martin, Gretchen. Miami, Florida. Bachelor of Science. (305) 235-0698, Gretchen1911@aol.com

Murphy, Brenda. Walton County, Georgia. Certified Nurtured Heart Specialist, Master of Arts in Psychology, Doctor of Divinity. 866-571-7990 (toll free), www.parentcoachingcenter.com, BrendaGACentre@comcast.net

Parkoff, Dana. Dallas/Plano, Texas. Certified Nurtured Heart Specialist, Bachelor of Arts in Communications, Certified K-12 Teacher. (214) 802-5471, dana@nurturedheartparenting.com, www.nurturedheartparenting.com

Redford, Susan. Yuma, Arizona. Certified Nurtured Heart Specialist, Master of Arts, Licensed Professional Counselor, Licensed Independent Substance Abuse Counselor. sjred51@hotmail.com

Schenkel, Shelah J. Springfield, Missouri. Certified Nurtured Heart Specialist, Master of Arts in Clinical Psychology, Licensed Professional Counselor. (417) 300-2489, shelahschenkel@yahoo.com

Shepherd-Campbell, Brenda. Spokane, Washington. Associate of Arts in Massage Therapy, Nurse's Assistant Registered. dbsmom@yahoo.com

Sherrod, Kathryn, Ph.D. Nashville, Tennessee. Certified Nurtured Heart Specialist, Psychologist. www.nashvilletherapy.com

Shober, Sherri. Rochester, Minnesota. Certified Nurtured Heart Specialist, Master of Arts in Elementary Education, Licensed Preschool and K-6 Teacher. (763) 560-9379, sherrisho@comcast.net, shobers@district279.org

Skinner, Cindy. West Chester, Ohio. Certified Nurtured Heart Specialist, Master in Social Work, Licensed Social Worker. (513) 644-1030

Small, Tammy. Bellevue, Washington. Certified Nurtured Heart Specialist, Master in Educational Psychology, Certified School Counselor. (425) 221-0171, tammyfsmall@gmail.com, www.nurturedheart.net

Thomas, Ellen. Champaign, Illinois. Bachelor of Science in Kinesiology, pursing Master of Science in School Counseling.

Wassmann, Karen. Miami, Florida. Certified Nurtured Heart Specialist, Licensed Clinical Social Worker. (305) 345-0156, KWassmann@AOL.com

Whitney, Erin. Houston, Texas, and Boulder, Colorado. Certified Nurtured Heart Specialist, Master of Arts in Clinical Psychology, Licensed Professional Counselor, Licensed Psychological Associate. (281) 728-7181, nurturedheartkids@yahoo.com, www.nurturedheartkids.com

Zola, Susan, Ed.D. Champaign, Illinois. Certified Nurtured Heart Specialist. (217) 351-3790, zolasu@champaignschools.org

RESOURCES

Nurtured Heart Approach Support Information
Three websites are available to those who seek information about the Nurtured Heart Approach:
www.EnergyParenting.com, www.DifficultChild.com and www.NurturingGreatness.net.

EnergyParenting.com is the online learning center for the Nurtured Heart Approach. It is a members-only website where parents, educators, coaches and therapists can quickly learn the approach's techniques and then continually hone their expertise through innovative learning modules, discussion forums, tele-seminars, as well as feature articles, products and services supporting the approach. Readers can join EnergyParenting.com at a **special reduced rate** by sending an e-mail to susan@EnergyParenting.com with the subject line: I want the "Friends of Howard Glasser" offer.

The other two sites – DifficultChild.com and Nurturing Greatness.net – both have research findings related to this topic, information about coaching and therapy services, information about Nurtured Heart workshops and Advanced Trainings, and information about creating training events for your organization.

Books on the Nurtured Heart Approach
The books listed below are available in most libraries and bookstores and from online sources. They also can be ordered at the Nurtured Heart Approach websites, www.DifficultChild.com or www.NurturingGreatness.net, or via a toll-free call to 800-311-3132.

- *Transforming the Difficult Child: The Nurtured Heart Approach* (1999) by Howard Glasser and Jennifer Easley.
- *101 Reasons to Avoid Ritalin Like the Plague AND One Great Reason Why It's Almost ALWAYS Unnecessary* (2005) by Howard Glasser with Melissa Lynn Block.
- *The Inner Wealth Initiative: The Nurtured Heart Approach for Educators* (2007) by Howard Glasser and Tom Grove with Melissa Lynn Block.

- *Transforming the Difficult Child Workbook – An Interactive Guide to the Nurtured Heart Approach* (2008) by Howard Glasser, Joann Bowdidge and Lisa Bravo.
- *All Children Flourishing: Igniting the Greatness of Our Children* (2008) by Howard Glasser with Melissa Lynn Block.

Audio-Visual Resources

Transforming the Difficult Child: The Nurtured Heart Approach Training Tapes are available on CD (audio only, 2.5 hours); on audiotape (audio only, 2.5 hours); on VHS (audio-visual, 2.5 hours); and on DVD (audio-visual, with a six-hour version and a four-hour version). These can be ordered via the websites and toll-free phone number listed above.